P. D. Evans.

Ex. Libris.

Book Tokens from
Dadley & Family, 13/8/91.

C000161701

FORMER SOLDIER
SEEKS
EMPLOYMENT

'GOOD OLD RONNIE'
IN COURT FIGHT

We want

BRAZIL last night officially asked Barbados to arrest the men they claim are responsible for kidnapping Ronald Biggs.

Charge d'Affaires Rohad Zero went to the Foreign Ministry in Bridgetown to make the request.

He named eight men: The skipper and crew of the yacht Nowcani Two — Thorfinn MacIver, Norman Boyle, Freddie Prime, Mark Algate, Anthony Marriage and American Greg Nelson

The other two were n security com-directors John and Patrick King.

from IAIN WALKER in BRIDGETOWN

HE GREAT ESCAPER   ...ted like a hero

ler, showstopping

Snatch squad chief:

BRAZIL W

peer ... and

ng Pres

FORMER SOLDIER
SEEKS
EMPLOYMENT

...nakes the am...

CA

ING

CUS

WE

NEW LUCAN

Possible experts say it ...d his ... could be ...rged with conspiracy if kidnap plot was hato... in Britain.

Miller, at present visiting Los Angeles, is on £2,500 bail on

John Miller
with
Gerry Brown

Continued from Page One

account

he and his with Mil-trip to a d last Fri-man said ng earl. the photo-just after two other boat.

'When we e camera I and ran knocking

was shot other men e fire. The

'Lucan' boat then sped off.

Suchet, who arrived back in London yesterday, said Miller was saved

from death by a bullet-proof vest

He added: "The whole thing was bizarre, but I'm convinced the shooting was not faked.

"I saw briefly a man with a mop of blond hair and a pretty droopy moustache."

His account is backed-up by a mystery bikini-clad blonde named Donna, who joined Miller's boat before it set sail from Miami.

She said last night: "I was told it was going to be a romantic cruise, then all hell broke loose with bullets whizzing around.

"Someone shouted to me 'keep your head' down and shut up! I ran below deck and hid under one of the bunks."

When the shooting stopped Donna went up on deck

His badly shakin seemed

'He but I trip out.'

Mille been have vincin

Such becom he sa were board the v

Late hyster that h shoot crew down him h

BIGGS LOSES
COURT FIGHT
FOR FREEDO

LORD
M
CAN'

MACMILLAN
LONDON

By IAN BALL in Bridgetown, Barba

THE latest chapter in the saga of Ronald Biggs was drawing to a close in

Copyright © John Miller 1989

All rights reserved. No reproduction, copy or transmission of this
publication may be made without written permission. No
paragraph of this publication may be reproduced, copied or
transmitted save with written permission or in accordance with
the provisions of the Copyright Act 1956 (as amended). Any
person who does any unauthorised act in relation to this
publication may be liable to criminal prosecution and civil
claims for damages.

First published 1989 by
MACMILLAN LONDON LIMITED
4 Little Essex Street London WC2R 3LF
and Basingstoke

Associated companies in Auckland, Delhi, Dublin, Gaborone,
Hamburg, Harare, Hong Kong, Johannesburg, Kuala Lumpur,
Lagos, Manzini, Melbourne, Mexico City, Nairobi, New York,
Singapore and Tokyo

A CIP catalogue record for this book is available from the
British Library.

ISBN 0-333-44900-2

Typeset by Wyvern Typesetting Ltd, Bristol, England
Printed by Billing and Sons Ltd, Worcester, England

Contents

This book is dedicated to:

Queen and Country, serving them gave me some great
   material;
the Brigade of Guards for teaching me to iron clothes
   properly;
Willie McGill, M.M. my first squad instructor;
President Sukarno for getting me posted to the Far East;
Freddie Prime, the giggling Guardsman;
Ronnie Biggs for two holidays in Rio;
Jack Slipper, thanks for the help, Jack;
Robin Wren, come out come out wherever you are;
HRH for the game of polo;
Alex Harvey, I wish you were here to see this Alex;
Levi Strauss for my genes;
Billy Idol for the Harley Davidson;
Arthur Scargill for doing for haircuts what Attila the Hun
   did for the Peace Movement;
the Scottish National Party, come on guys, get real;
the British tabloid press, without whose help etc., etc.;
Philip Finn who said my marriage would never last, it'll be
   eight years next year, Phil;
Jamaica, shame it isn't run properly;
Ewan Lawrie, your jetty was better than Alec's bridge;
Kim Basinger for the great weekend;
the County Bar, Almada Street, Hamilton;
Gavin Goodwin, the first man I knew who took business
   calls in a pub;
Tam Lindsay, for teaching me, among other things,
   Regimental police work;
Danny White who lost his life in the Falklands campaign;
Sean Sullivan, if he had money people would call him
   eccentric but he's much more than that;
anybody with a 38DD, please call;
my in-laws, keep looking, you'll eventually see the joke;
my daughter Lisa, why don't you ever write?;
Butch Stone who knows what really happened to JFK;
the gay club in Soho, it still hurts;
the Rainbow Bar and Grill, what can I say?;
the French Resistance, 'allo, 'allo;
Sir Hugh Fraser, when he went so did my credit at Harrods;
Fast Eddie Tobin, remember Ridge Farm?;
Chris Glen for taking me to Tokyo;
Big Daft Shape for starring in my home movie;

Colonel Ross for a great night at the Macclesfield Rugby
    Club;

Lieutenant Leaske for my first appearance in court in
    Glasgow;

Norrie Hughes, it's OK I didn't want to be an NCO first
    time round anyway;

Steve Barron, who wouldn't be where he is today if he'd
    taken my advice;

Zelda Barron for great breakfasts at Powis Terrace;

Andy McCracken, go on, Andy, have a drink;

Andy Dunlop, the only man I know who can sit up while
    lying down;

the Pipes and Drums of the 1st Battalion, Scots Guards.
    Nobody does it better;

Alex Duthart, who I worked with. Sorry it took so long to
    find out how great you were;

Eric Cronfeld, Mr Sensitivity;

Bob Quine, give up the Valium, Bob;

Lou Reed. I never said your wife was fat but I know who
    did;

Jack Healey of Amnesty International. It's a great idea
    Jack but it'll never catch on;

the Provisional IRA. Come out and fight like men, you
    bastards;

Jackie Kennedy. If you'd played your cards right you could
    have been editing this book;

my PE teacher at Gresham House School, who only had one
    leg but was a great laugh;

Janette Bowman. She knows what for;

the estate agent who sold me my house. You knew the roof
    leaked, didn't you?;

Spike, who shared so many mad times with me. I know
    you're out there, get in touch;

Mae McFarlane, spend 1s.6d., reach new heights;

John David Kalodor for his exquisite taste in women and
    being slightly right of Genghis Kahn. Give them hell,
    John;

Steve Sterling, who always thought this could be done. He
    provided enthusiasm and listened patiently for hours;

Jerry Brown, it was third time lucky. I should have trusted
    my instincts and gone to you first.

my wife Sarah, who has been more than I could have hoped
    for in every department as a wife, a mistress and a
    mother and for giving me two beautiful children, Kate
    and James.

Prologue

It was the kind of discreet, private office the Chairman preferred to use when he was making sneaky personal deals. I'd expected to be invited to the plush executive suite near Buckingham Palace but there were probably too many secretaries there who were paid to keep a wary eye on the Chairman's visitors and to listen out for the door of the cocktail cabinet swinging open before midday. The executive suite was fine for entertaining heads of governments and presidents and princes, but we needed somewhere the Chairman wouldn't be interrupted by awkward members of his board of directors, or share-holders demanding to know what the hell was going on, or flunkeys and officials of Her Majesty arriving to make special requests on his time. This little penthouse tucked away on top of a department store, spitting distance from the Soviet Embassy, was ideal. It had only one direct telephone line and an extension answered by a personal assistant who never screened the callers too closely and didn't give a shit what time of day the first cocktails were served.

In the penthouse we could spread out the maps and plans in privacy and the Chairman could sip on a man-sized gin to help get his mind into slightly sharper focus.

'So, you want to kidnap Ronnie Biggs?' he asked.

'Kidnap . . .? Kidnap . . .? Christ no,' I protested. 'Come on, I wouldn't get involved in anything like that. And

I wouldn't be asking a decent, respectable man like yourself to put up money for anything low-down or criminal.'

The Chairman laughed. He poured himself another drink and flopped back down in his swivel chair. 'Cut the bullshit, John. If I was totally decent and respectable you wouldn't be here in the first place. You've got to come up with a better reason than that.'

I had plenty of time. He had cleared his appointments diary for the next couple of hours. I'd start off by appealing to his sense of fairness and moral indignation – you know, 'Why should a convicted, violent criminal and jailbreaker like Ronnie Biggs be allowed to live in freedom in Brazil giving the finger to British justice?' That sort of thing.

We were talking serious money, so I wasn't going to rush anything. The sales pitch would start by getting the Chairman wound up about the sheer outrage of it all. Ronnie Biggs had been a ringleader of a diabolical gang who had ambushed and robbed a Royal Mail train: theft from the Royal Mail, capital 'R', capital 'M'. It's got a ring of treason to it and the Chairman was well connected with royalty. He regularly sipped sherry with the Queen at Buckingham Palace garden parties and he was a night-clubbing, gin-and-tonic drinking buddy of her sister, Princess Margaret.

I could see the message was sinking in.

Then there was the attack on the train driver who was beaten senseless. Vicious and brutal, the Chairman agreed. The Chairman was a staunch law 'n' order man. And what about Biggs's escape from prison and his snivelling sanctuary in Brazil? Even when those dogged, decent detectives of Scotland Yard tracked him down to Rio and flew there on the instructions of Her Majesty's Government, the double-dealing Brazilians had refused to hand him over on the shameless technicality that he had fathered an illegitimate Brazilian kid while he was on the run. The Chairman was gripping his gin glass just a little tighter. Bloody foreigners, dagos, banditos, all of them.

I flipped open a folder of press cuttings, with photos showing a sun-tanned Biggs cavorting on a beach with long-legged, topless Latino beauties giggling in the background. The Chairman put his glass down and picked up the cuttings. He walked over to the window to see them in a better light, squinting in disgust at the grinning Biggs and then lingering absentmindedly on the figures of the girls from Ipanema. Outside the penthouse, it was a cold and wet November afternoon and trudging Londoners were fighting their way through puddles of rainwater and bone-chilling winds. The folder of press photos showed blue skies, golden sands and Biggs, posing with arms raised like a boxing champion, wearing a white sweatshirt with the crest of England, lions and roses, sewn on the breast.

I kept my mouth shut and walked over to the cocktail cabinet to help myself to another drink and just wait a few seconds for the Chairman to savour the insult. He went back to his desk, sat down and spread out the whole file of press photos and maps and plans with a sweep of his hand. Then he clenched his fist.

'You're right, John, it's a bloody liberty. Lucky bastard doesn't deserve it. But short of kidnapping him there's nothing you nor I or anyone else can do about it.' His blood pressure was up and gin was doing its job. Now was the time to appeal to his sense of the absurd and ridiculous.

'I'm going after him, and it's not a kidnap,' I said. 'It's a citizen's arrest.'

'Citizen's arrest . . .? Oh, I see. Now that's different. That could be, well, nearly sort of legal, couldn't it?' The Chairman was thinking hard, nodding slowly.

'I snatch him from Brazil and take him to a decent, loyal island in the Caribbean where they've still got some respect for British law and he'll get deported right back to a British jail.' I was laying it on heavy now. 'That's where people like him belong. I mean look at him now, hanging around beaches all day long, pawing those skinny bimbos with big tits. Probably spends the night snorting cocaine – it's dirt cheap and damn near legal out there – and bedding women two at a time. Thinks he's some kinda hero while the rest of us have to work for a living.'

Ronnie Biggs never had a board of directors or whining shareholders to answer to, or Department of Trade inspectors poking their noses into his bank accounts, or unreasonable casino bosses refusing to take his post-indated cheques. The Chairman did, and he could just taste the unfairness of it all so much that, right at that minute, he would have captured Biggs himself and swum the Atlantic back to Wandsworth Prison, dragging the Train Robber by the hair.

'I've got some good, loyal army buddies who'll make the trip with me,' I told him, 'and I've got some senior people at Scotland Yard backing me unofficially all the way. They've told me exactly which island to land him on, to make sure he doesn't wriggle off the hook with some legal trickery. If I snatch him and just hand him over to the law, how can that be a kidnap? It's a public service, that's what it is.'

He poured a couple of drinks for both of us.

'Get him back here, John. Make him pay for what he's done. How much do you need?'

I ran a finger down the itemised list of scheduled air tickets, hotel expenses, jet hire, yacht charter, until I reached the bottom line. It was petty cash to a man who had gambled and lost £2 million at roulette tables in less than two years.

'I'll have it for you by the end of the week,' he said. 'It's coming out of my own funds, nothing to do with the business accounts, so you've got to give me a couple of days.'

4

We shook on it and as we walked to the door, the Chairman put his arm round my shoulder and asked the question he should have asked before we even sat down to our first drink.

'By the way, what's in this for you, John?'

'I just want to get even with the bastard,' I said.

'Oh,' he said, and he looked as if he had no idea what I meant. Then he got that faraway look again, just as he'd done when he saw the beach pictures, and he seemed happy that he knew why I wanted to go 8,000 miles and play the Avenging Angel. He didn't really have a clue.

Then the clincher.

'What's in it for me, John?'

'The satisfaction of knowing you've served your Queen and country,' I said. He didn't look as if he thought he was getting value for money.

'I couldn't take any of the credit for it, John. In fact I wouldn't want to have my name connected with it in any way. It would have to be a secret between us.'

'O K,' I assured him. 'After I pull this off you'll have first call on me to do a personal job for you anywhere in the world.'

'Any kind of job?'

'Within the law,' I said, and then I thought about the plot we had just agreed and changed that to, '. . . well, within reason.'

I caught the private elevator down to ground level and walked across the street. Waiting to hail a cab, I looked up to the top of the building and the Chairman was at the penthouse window gazing down into the street. He looked as if he was dreaming up a better version of the plot: put on a bit of weight, get plastic surgery, the hairline and colour was just about right, get John Miller to make the switch between him and Ronnie Biggs. Wandsworth Prison wouldn't be punishment enough for Biggs, he could have the board of directors and the shareholders, the penthouse and executive suite in Knightsbridge and the estate in Scotland. And the Chairman would take his chances with the beach and the bimbos.

Two days later I walked into an office in Glasgow and told the secretary the Chairman was expecting me. She buzzed through on an intercom and said: 'Sir Hugh, a Mr John Miller is here to see you.'

Sir Hugh Fraser, the Chairman of Harrods, was ready and waiting when I went into his private apartments.

'Just one more question, John,' he said and I wondered if he was going to pull out of the project.

'Sure, Hugh, what do you want to know?'

'The media, the papers and television, they'll still call this a kidnapping, won't they?'

Well, he should know, I thought. He owns two of Britain's most profitable daily and evening newspapers.

'What's the penalty in Brazil for kidnapping?' Sir Hugh asked.

'About a hundred years in jail, that's just a guess. And the same for making a citizen's arrest if the Brazilians don't see the funny side of it.'

'What about being just a . . . uhh . . . partner in . . . uhh . . . a conspiracy to make a citizen's arrest?'

'Just like being there doing the actual snatch. But don't worry, Hugh, if the Brazilians won't deport a convicted robber back to Britain to finish a prison stretch, do you think the Queen is going to let her Government deport the boss of Harrods, her personal storekeeper, to face a rigged trial in Brazil just because he did his patriotic duty?'

'Uhmm . . . just to be on the safe side John, you won't mention my name to anyone, will you?'

'No problem, Hugh.'

The money was double-wrapped inside brown envelopes in a green and gold plastic Harrod's shopping bag, service and discretion assured. He didn't ask for a receipt or an IOU and I caught the next plane back to London.

It was the second time in two years I had asked somebody to back me with cash to capture Ronnie Biggs. The first time had ended with Ronnie leering at me as I was bundled into the back of a Brazilian paddy wagon on my way to jail while he strolled back to the beach. I had been tossed into a cell, humiliated and then deported. And I had blown £50,000 of someone else's cash in the attempt. My pride had been really, really badly hurt. I never thought I'd get a second chance. Now I had the money to go after him again and this time there would be no slip-ups. I was running over and over again in my mind the scene where I'd be saying to the Great Train Robber, 'Hello, Ronnie, remember me? I swore I'd get you sooner or later.'

<u>Army</u>

The old recruiting slogan was 'It's a Man's Life in the Regular Army.' It's a very simple advertisement and very effective – a bit like the old song 'We joined the Navy to see the World', which is followed by the line, 'And what did we see? We saw the Sea!'. There are a lot of jokes about 'It's a Man's Life in the Regular Army' as well, but I didn't know them when I first tried to join up in my teens. I genuinely believed the Army was a man's life and a man's life was what I wanted. It would get me out of Motherwell.

Motherwell is a steel and engineering town in Central Scotland – strictly heavy industry and spit and sawdust Scottish pubs with none of the glamour of wicked Glasgow twenty miles to the west, or the culture and poshness of Edinburgh fifty miles to the east. I was born there in February 1945.

I grew up earlier than most boys. At least that's what I think. I guess some of my contemporaries think they're the ones who grew up early. If growing up means becoming middle-aged overnight, then maybe they're right. But by my definition of adulthood, I grew up fast. That was partly because I just matured early but also because I never knew my father. He was killed before I was born.

My father was a bomb aimer in the Royal Air Force during the war. His plane was shot down over Holland coming back from a raid on the Ruhr. He had been in the police force before, which had made him exempt from military service, but he wasn't prepared to sit out the war as a policeman, so he volunteered. I get the impression he was that sort of man – he had a great sense of right and wrong. He would have hated sitting around at home while his mates were off getting shot at.

He was very much a man's man too. He boxed for Scotland and for Great Britain. I still have trunks full of his medals and cups and belts. He was smaller than me, about five foot ten to my six foot two and he was a middleweight whereas I boxed at light heavyweight. They called him 'The amateur Len Harvey' – Len Harvey being just about the best British professional of the day. He was a very good boxer – not a great puncher, but a very clever fighter. There was even a cup named after him. I wanted to box for the cup myself – it went to the winner of the Scottish middleweight championships and I wanted to win it for my mother, but I couldn't make the weight.

My mother lived on till the spring of 1987 and all through more than forty years of widowhood she always talked of my father and she always had his photograph on display. I often wonder what our lives would have been like if he had lived, but I had a very happy childhood.

We lived in this tenement building, my mother, my grandmother and myself. My mother was working as a typist for a company that made air rifles; my grandmother wasn't working. I trotted dutifully off to Knowtop Primary School when I was four-and-a-half, but my real education began a few years later. When I was seven years old, I sailed away on the P & O liner, the *Edinburgh Castle*. My aunt and uncle had gone off to Rhodesia a year or so before and they wrote to tell my mother what a great place Rhodesia was – great opportunity, wonderful country, lots of work and lots of single men. I'm sure the single men had a lot to do with it! I had three years in Africa. Magic. The space, the freedom, the animals, the chance to be on your own. It was great.

Soon after we arrived to live in the little town of Nkana, my mother remarried. My stepfather was called John MacDonald and like my uncle he worked for Rokana Corporation which was a big American mining outfit. They seemed to own Nkana and the twin town next door, Kitwe. It was a strange existence. We had our own house and servants and everything revolved round the golf club and the yacht club and the polo field. Even as a kid who found it a wrench to adapt to this new world away from the cramped rain-sodden streets of Motherwell, I could see it had attractions for grown-ups who hadn't a hope of such things as servants or golf and polo and yachts if they'd stayed home in Britain.

I was soon growing up as a junior jungle boy. After school finished each day I'd roam into the bush, the little White Hunter, trapping bush babies and monkeys and birds. The black garden boy taught me how to skin snakes, like the Gaboon Viper. The natives used to wait till they saw the snake going down a hole, then they'd grab it by the tail and crack it like a whip. The flick action killed the snake. I just used a forked stick and bashed them up. I wasn't sure how to cure the skins. Saltpetre didn't really do the job. The natives had this incredible stuff they'd made up which didn't only cure the snake skins but left them very supple. Mine were so stiff you could use them as cricket bats. When I finally managed to cure them properly, I made them into hatbands, Crocodile Dundee style, and I covered sheaths for my knife in snakeskin too. But maybe I was growing up too wild and it was too good to last.

One day my mother's cousin rang from Scotland saying, 'There's this wonderful boarding school . . .' It was run by an eccentric headmaster with two daughters and a wife who was just as off-the-wall as the rest of the family. He had had a school in Ayrshire called Gresham House School and he'd moved on to take Lord Hamilton's estate.

It is a huge place – big turrets, a moat, drawbridges, secret passages, the whole shebang. They used it recently as the location for a Robert Louis Stevenson movie, *Kidnapped*. And my mother decided I should go there.

In many ways it was a completely useless place to send me in the hope of turning me into a young gentleman, but the environment really appealed. The grounds were incredible: some parts were out of bounds because there were dangerous canyons and gorges; there was a Japanese garden with a little Japanese house and waterfall and seven or eight hundred different sorts of flowers and shrubs; there were those Japanese trees you can punch and the bark is soft like flesh. I used to go outside the grounds, into forbidden territory, whenever I could, until the inevitable happened and I got caught. The headmaster was one of those devout believers in discipline who always carried a bamboo cane up his sleeve.

'Right, boy!' he roared, 'You've been out of bounds, boy! You come over here, boy!'

So I said: 'No, sir, I haven't.'

And he said: 'You have, bend over.' And he whacked me with the cane and then said, 'Do you know how I know you've been out of bounds?'

'No, sir,' I said.

'Because you have burrs on your socks,' he told me. The burrs only grew outside the grounds. That was my first lesson in fieldcraft behind enemy lines.

All of the teachers at Gresham House seemed to be the oddities of the Scottish educational system, even the sportsmaster, a retired naval commander. He only had one leg. I mean, can you believe it, a sportsmaster with only one leg?

I didn't learn much from academic subjects, but I came out knowing which knife and fork to use and I'd met people from decent homes.

Maybe I exaggerate about the low educational value of

Gresham House, because after two years I did manage to pass my eleven-plus and I went to Dalziel High School. My leaving report from Gresham said, 'If John applied himself in the classroom with the same fervour and zest he brings to his sport he would be a brilliant academic.' Well, I'm afraid I've never really managed to bring that sort of enthusiasm to academic work unless I can see its relevance. My favourite subject was Geography because that was about travel and faraway places. I could recite every capital city in the world off pat. I still can and I love to travel whenever I can.

One interesting option at Dalziel High School was the choice between a commercial subject or Woodwork. The Woodwork teacher was a maniac whose main pleasure seemed to be throwing hammers and chisels at his class. But Commercial Study, which was typing and shorthand, was a different ballgame. That class was full of stunning girls in tight sweaters. And halfway through lessons you used to break for a cup of tea. So naturally I said, 'You can keep Woodwork.' The other blokes all thought Woodwork or Metalwork was what the lads did. It was macho. But it didn't make sense to me. I wanted to be in there among the women and the cups of tea. I've never understood what was so macho about having a hard time.

Not that I had any problem with my masculinity. I was playing centre three-quarter in the first XV. Rugby was a religion in that part of Scotland and the centre three-quarter was a glamour position. I always knew with a rugby player whether he was a forward or a back. The forwards' bellies hung out and their socks were round their ankles. The backs had combed hair and no beer guts. At centre three-quarter in the Dalziel High School First XV, I felt I was part of an élite.

None of that improved my academic qualifications, though, so I left school at sixteen and went to work in the personnel office at the steelworks. It was incredibly dull.

My mum wanted me to settle down into a nice, safe, white-collar job, with wife, kids, the whole bit. It was not what I had in mind.

They were all back in Scotland by then – my mum, stepfather and grandmother. My parents had a small-holding outside town but I lived with my grandmother in her little house opposite the church in Motherwell. I used to go out to the farm occasionally, of course. They had about a hundred pigs and a lot of Victoria plums, straw-berries, raspberries, blackcurrants. There was the added attraction of a gambling school near the farm. It was called 'The Canyon' and the main game was Pitch and Toss. The police used to raid it from time to time but the gamblers had a system of lookouts which kept them mostly safe and I'd take bags of fruit to sell to them. On Sundays I'd be there all day. Men would gamble the family pay packet away. There were drunks, there were fights, and there I was flogging pears and strawberries to these drunken men. It was how I made some extra money and I loved it.

The other excitement was the Majestic Ballroom. I had one of those weird suits with the half belt and vents in the back and covered buttons and French seams. That was the fashion and the Majestic was where I went to meet girls. It was also where they had live rock 'n' roll gigs. I remember Screaming Lord Sutch arriving on stage in a coffin. Another time Gene Vincent came and there was a huge crowd, shoving and pushing. Fransie McCabe, one of the local hard men, very deliberately got up on stage and sat there while Gene Vincent did his act. It was a menacing reminder to all the regulars at the Majestic that even a big star like Gene Vincent was only a fleeting visitor on Fransie McCabe's patch. That was the sort of gesture I admired.

Even in my teens I had developed a taste for the wild. I liked to be my own man. I liked gambling dens, I liked excitement, I liked women, I liked a life that most people fight shy of even if they enjoy it when they see it in the movies. Most people seem to be quite content to live their lives in armchairs. They'll grumble and fret but the basic truth is they're too damned scared to get out and do a bit of real living. I always wanted more from life than that. I knew there were people out there in the big world having some fun and some excitement and taking some risks and I wanted to be out there with them. The army slogan seemed to promise everything I was looking for, and it would get me away from the personnel department of the steelworks and save me from the prospect of a nine to five job, a wife, two kids and a mortgage.

I chose the Scots Guards because they're the pride of Scotland. There are other famous Scots regiments – the Black Watch, the Royal Scots Greys, the Argylls – but there's nothing quite like the Scots Guards. My uncle had been in the Guards too – that may have had something to do with my choice. He used to tell me horror stories about how they were made to swim in freezing cold water at four in the morning and how they were the toughest troops in the whole army. I heard stories about the Guards regiments marching in perfect lines on to the beaches at Dunkirk to wait for the boats to take them off under German bombardment. And how they lined up on the beaches in three ranks and then whitened their belts and polished their boots under fire because it was important for the Guards always to look their best.

The regiment was formed in 1642 to go to Belfast, to put down the Troubles. It's quite ironic to think they're still being sent there and they're still being ordered to put down the Troubles. They've always been infantry, and as everyone knows it's the poor bloody infantry who are the ones who do most of the actual fighting. And because the Scots Guards have always been an ace regiment they've always been where the fighting's fiercest. Right up to the

Falklands War. They have always won the enemy's respect. After the Battle of Waterloo, Napoleon said that trying to charge at the Scots Guards was like charging at a stone wall.

I was attracted to them because they were the best and it was a challenge even to get into the regiment. They're the Queen's personal bodyguard. The men are some of the best Jocks in Scotland while the officers are some of the grandest gentry. A Guards' officer has to have a private income before he's allowed to join the regiment and he has to pay for all his own uniforms. There's this old story about the Guards' officer posted abroad on active service who was told to take only the basic kit. 'What's basic kit?' he asks. 'Dinner jacket and toothbrush,' says the Commanding Officer. If it's not a true story then it should be because Guards' officers have an amazing sense of style. They're the ultimate British gentlemen and even if they sometimes seem to come out of a novel by P.G. Wodehouse, they hardly ever give you a dull moment.

I joined them in 1962 when I was seventeen-and-a-half. I'd tried earlier when I was sixteen but my mother refused to sign the documents. She was very upset when a big sergeant arrived at my house one day with me in a Landrover, because I'd convinced him she'd sign. She told him to get lost. I wanted to be a boy soldier but you couldn't do that without your mum's permission. So I waited another eighteen months and tried again. I signed on for three years and caught the train from Glasgow to London with a young boy called Dougal McMillan, who came from Tarbert near Campbeltown and had never been out of Scotland before. It was amazing to watch him on escalators and the Underground. He was like Crocodile Dundee in New York.

At the beginning of your life in the Guards you get chased around. The authorities, who in this case are the senior

16

non-commissioned officers, make your life as mean and miserable as they possibly can. The idea is to give you a first taste of what the Army's like. Everything is done in double time. A depot is the showplace of every regiment: that's where it starts, that's where they train you. So they insist on higher standards there than when you go to the battalion. When you go to the battalion, things are more relaxed. You don't have to walk at exactly 172 paces a minute. You're down to 120 paces. My hair was cut so short it was like sandpaper. My scalp looked like Bob Geldof's chin.

I had a trained soldier as a permanent escort. He was only the same rank as me, a Guardsman, but if I wanted to leave or enter my room I had to come to attention outside my door and ask: 'Permission to enter the room, trained soldier. Permission to leave the room, trained soldier.' We used to think these men were wonderful. It was only later that we realised they weren't wonderful at all – they were wimps and deadbeats who were no use in the battalion itself. But what does a recruit know?

There are five regiments of Foot Guards: Grenadier Guards, Coldstream Guards, Scots Guards, Irish Guards and Welsh Guards. They all have red tunics and bearskins but things like buttons and plumes are different. In the old days these distinguishing marks helped to identify different units on the field of battle. The Scots Guards have tunic buttons grouped in threes, a thistle on their collar, and no plume on their bearskin. That was because when there were only three regiments of Guards, they formed the middle. The Grenadiers to their right had a white plume and the Coldstreams on their left wore red. This was so that the Generals Commanding – who naturally were always behind their men – could determine from the rear where the individual regiments were.

All the drill manuals for armies throughout the world, including America, are based on Brigade of Guards' drill.

That's because Guards' drill is the oldest and best. When I was with them you could see it in action on public duties at Buckingham Palace, at the Tower of London, St James's Palace and the Bank of England. The best of all was at the Queen's Birthday Parade every summer when we trooped the Colour before Her Majesty on Horse Guards' Parade.

I spent two years after the depot on these 'Public Duties'. It was strange, dressing up like a toy soldier and being gawped at by the tourists. In those days we were in sentry-boxes outside Buckingham Palace — inside the railings. They've moved the Guards behind the railings now because the tourists were giving them such a hard time. I've had women try to cut the buttons off my tunic and stick love letters with telephone numbers down my front. Ambitious homosexuals would try and touch me up. I've even had apples stuck on the end of my bayonet. But you're not allowed to say or do anything. We managed to perfect the art of saying 'Fuck off' out of the corners of our mouths without moving our lips at all. It was that old Guards' discipline at work again. You had to remain steady under fire. Mind you, if you could hear what was being said under our breaths you'd be quite shocked. At the Queen's Birthday Parade, whenever there was a really fabulous bird in the crowd, the word used to get passed along the ranks: 'Three o'clock, just under the War Memorial, dark glasses, straw hat, yellow dress, great pair of tits.'

People often fainted on that parade. You were standing to attention for hours in that terrible stuffy uniform, so it was hardly surprising. But it was a matter of honour not to faint first, so if one of your mates passed out, the men on either side would hold him up by his belt until we got word that a man in one of the other regiments had fallen over. Then you could let your own man go. You had to keep up appearances at all costs. There was one famous occasion when an officer was marching his picket from the barracks to the Bank of England and, because the traffic was bad, he realised he was going to be late for changing the Guard. So he marched his men into the Tube station, bought twenty-four tickets and took his picket to Bank station on the Tube. Can you imagine the reaction of the other passengers when they saw this detachment of Guards marching down the escalator, two abreast, bayonets fixed with an officer in front with a drawn sword?

Originally I signed on for a three-year engagement and I was paid a pathetic four pounds a week. But for some unaccountable reason, if I signed on for nine years the pay shot up to something like nine pounds a week, so I changed the deal to nine years. It seemed only sensible. I wasn't just being mercenary because it wasn't long before I really started to enjoy it and I could see myself staying beyond those original three years. I'd always been an athletic person. I'd played rugby, I'd boxed, I'd run. Now I was being paid to do all three. In that sense it was like being a professional sportsman. But I was also keen on soldiering – perhaps at heart I really am a warrior – and I was getting paid to do that too. I'd fired rifles in Africa – .410 and 12-gauge shotguns on the farm at home – but nothing like the high velocity 7.62mm we used in the Army. It was exciting.

Before they gave us our guns they gave us our boots. Proper sense of military priorities! The brand new boots had little pimples on the leather. You got a hot spoon and burned all the pimples off until the leather was smooth. And then you put layers and layers of polish on and you spat on them and rubbed them until you could see your face in them. The whole boot, the heel, the toe. I'll never forget this one guy who was ordered: 'Go down to the boiler-house and burn your boots.' They used to shovel coal in '62, there was no oil-fired central heating and it was bitter cold that January. So he went down and opened the boiler door and threw his boots in.

Guards sergeants used to play hell with squaddies. Us new recruits were so green, so wet behind the ears, that we made it easy for them. I remember just after we got our guns, our sergeant said we must treat our rifles as our best friend. We had to go everywhere with them just like we'd go everywhere with our best friend. We even had to sleep with our rifles, just as we'd sleep with our best friends. I wasn't too sure about this especially as my best friends tended to be guys, so I slept without my rifle. It was the wrong decision. That bastard sergeant was in at 3 a.m. searching every bed. Everyone not sleeping with his rifle was pushed outside into the snow and forced to do press-ups!

They'd say: 'Any football players here?' We were so green we'd all chorus: 'Yes, Sarn't Major, yes, Sarn't Major, three bags full, Sarn't Major.' 'All right, you cut the grass, you rake up the grass, you mark the lines in the field.' Or: 'Anybody cold in here?' 'Oh yes, Sarn't, I'm freezing.' 'All right, go and shovel that coal in the boiler-house.'

We had a sergeant called Willie McGill, who later won a Military Medal in Borneo. He was a great inspiration to me and what they now call a role model. Or even a father substitute, which, as you may have suspected already, is something I may have been looking for throughout much of my life. He used to whack me on the knuckles with a cane on cold mornings when I wasn't really curling my fingers the way I was supposed to. He'd kick me when I was on the firing range and I wasn't getting my arse moving. He was tough, he was hard. But everything he was telling me to do, he could do himself almost by instinct. And I used to say, 'I want to be just like him.' Years later I was finally given my sergeant's stripes and I had a big lump in my throat thinking, 'I've finally made it, I'm a sergeant in the Guards' depot', which is the highest accolade you can award a non-commissioned officer.

Parents would come up to me and say: 'Thank you, Sarn't, for turning my son into a man.' But what made me feel really proud was that I'd gone from just looking up to Willie McGill to being – I hope – just like him.

But that didn't happen at first. In the beginning I fell into bad company. I met Norrie Hughes. Apart from Willie McGill, Norrie was one of the biggest influences in my life. He had just come back from Kenya and I'd just arrived at the battalion after twenty-two weeks at the depot, during which I never got outside camp or wore civilian clothes. Norrie Hughes was a Guardsman too, after nine years in the Army. He'd had rank but he'd lost it – been busted. The first time Norrie came into my room, he said: 'I want you to have a look at these boots. These boots have been in the northern Frontier District, they've been in Kenya, they've been in Kahawa, they've been in Gilgil and in Mozambique and Mombasa and as a rare privilege, because I can see you're a promising lad, I'm gonna let you clean them. And because I like the look of you, I'm gonna let you lend me three pounds to go out tonight. In fact, I'll do better than that. I'm gonna take you out with me.' All bullshit, I know, but I was very young and I fell for it.

In the bar I sat with Norrie and the old lags – away from the other new boys. I became part of a little group of able, intelligent men who, for one reason or another, all said, 'Sod the system'.

Norrie was on the boxing team. So was I. And so was Fred Prime. Fred was an old soldier too. He actually led the great Guards' Brigade strike. They were doing three and four guards a week but there were only 200 men in the battalion and there should have been 600. They shouldn't really have been doing Public Duty at all. So they all went absent without leave. I don't think Fred was the brains behind the rebellion. I think someone put him up to it. But he had the muscle and the personality to make others follow him, so he was the ringleader. It caused a terrible furore in the press and brought discredit on the regiment.

So, those were the people I hung around with in my early days with the battalion: the heavy drinkers and the troublemakers. Norrie Hughes went on to become one of the regiment's top instructors and a senior NCO, but then we were the Awkward Squad. I was the best recruit when I left the Guards' depot. I was a squad leader, I was the recruit most destined to succeed. I was playing rugby for the Guards' depot, I was boxing for the Guards' depot. My personal record, which you have to sign so you can see what they put, said: 'This man should be a non-commissioned officer as soon as possible.' And I just blew it. I suppose I really wasn't ready to take on responsibility at that point, but then in 1964 the battalion was posted to Malaya.

They put a notice on the bulletin board saying: 'Anybody with a knowledge of dogs report to the Company Sergeant Major.' Well, of course I loved dogs, so myself and another guy that I became very close to, Charlie Nash, reported to the CSM. The sergeant major said: 'What knowledge of dogs do you have, Guardsman?' I said: 'Well, I was brought up on a farm, Sarn't, I've always had animals. I've trained sheep dogs before.' He said to Nash: 'Nash?' And Nash said, 'I used to bet on the greyhounds all the time, Sarn't.' We both got the jobs. The Army has never been too fussy about qualifications.

My own experience of dogs had included a couple of bitter-sweet relationships where I had mastered them but they had also been responsible for teaching me a few things about my own character. Growing up in Africa, I had kept a Rhodesian ridgeback called Tarzan. Big, big dog. Some of the other kids had party pieces they'd do – a song, a dance, a card trick, an impersonation. Tarzan and I had a circus routine. He'd sit on one stool and jump to another one. I'd get him to sit up on his back legs and roll over. He was an intelligent dog and I wouldn't like to say who taught who. We learned a great deal from each other.

And the finale of our act was when I took hold of his mouth and opened up his jaws and put my head in, pretending he was a lion. We were tremendous friends and had a great trust and respect for each other. He used to come and meet me at school and carry my school-bag home. Beautiful big dog, he died later when I was back in Britain at boarding school. Poisoned. Someone had put out bait to kill a jackal or wild dog and Tarzan ate it and died from something they call Stuttgart's Disease.

I had a Border collie a while later, on the farm in Scotland, but I had to shoot him when he started worrying sheep. That was a very profound moment in my life and not at all a nice experience. There was no question the dog would have to be put down. My Uncle Hugh was going to do it to spare my young feelings but I suddenly realised that it was my responsibility. He was my dog and if he had to be put down, then I was the person who had to shoot him. I hated doing it but it was necessary and it was a sort of watershed in my life, like losing my virginity. It was the first time I'd killed, and I'd killed something I loved.

There were four of us in the dog training team. Me, Charlie, Arthur Scott from the Drums Company (pipes and drums) and Eddie Meredith from a company of Irish Guards. A corporal called Bob Guthrie was put in charge of the team. And we went out to Johore Baharu, to the Jungle Warfare School, to No. 2 War Dog Training Unit.

Training dogs with the Army wasn't the sort of thing you see on television. It's not quite Phil Drabble in a cloth cap on the Pennines, let alone Barbara Woodhouse with a poodle in her backyard. It was a six-month course. The dogs were mainly black labradors though there were some German shepherds and a few crossbreeds. Mine was an untrained labrador called Lucky and we trained together which was a big advantage because it meant that we really got to know each other. The basis of the early training was tracking human quarry and the absolutely vital thing was getting to know your dog well enough to recognise when he'd found someone. Dogs react in a number of different ways – they may sit, or 'point' or just cock their ears. It was absolutely vital that the handler recognised those signs. Otherwise he'd stumble straight into an ambush.

The handler always had to be the master, but the dog must never be allowed to experience defeat. In training, the dog always beat off the guy and the guy always retreated. And the dog thought: 'Done it again.' Eventually the dog became so confident he didn't know the meaning of getting hurt. But only his handler told the dog what to do.

After about three months we moved on to crowd control. They'd take fifty guys and say, 'You guys are the enemy. I want you to give this dog and this handler a hard time.' They'd put you in a small street, you'd put the dog on an 18-foot line and just work it across the street. Sometimes the guys would get fired up and start throwing rocks at you. They'd have sticks, they'd be yelling, just like a real crowd. It would get to the point where they'd hit you with a few things and you'd begin to lose your rag and let the dog nip a few of them – just to show them who was in charge. There used to be these incredible scenes. Nobody'd want to be in the front because the guys at the back would push them towards the dogs, and the dogs bit. So the men in the front were trying to retreat and the men at the back were trying to advance. It was a holy shambles sometimes.

The first time we used the dogs was up on the Thai border. Eddie Meredith and I were called out one day when this lunatic escaped from a local bin in Johore. He'd been gone for a couple of days which meant the track was quite difficult to follow. Worse, they didn't tell us this guy had elephantiasis, which meant his legs and arms were all swollen up to the most enormous size. I tracked him for

24

about 4,000 yards after which my dog was getting tired. We were coming to some heavy fern and bracken and you could see where our man had obviously pushed himself through. So I said to Eddie, 'Put your dog on,' which meant that Eddie took his dog's collar off and put on a harness. That means the dog knows it's time to work and gets down to some serious tracking. I followed behind while Eddie and his dog Butch started to track through the ferns and bracken. Eddie was crawling along on all fours.

Suddenly I heard this screaming. He had come face to face with a really ghastly apparition. Our quarry was sitting propped up against a tree, so swollen he looked like the Michelin man. He was extremely dead. There were maggots crawling out of his nose and his eyes, and above all there was this truly terrible smell of putrefaction. He must have been dead for at least twenty-four hours. No wonder Eddie was screaming!

I went to Borneo with the dogs during the Indonesian emergency but that was a surprisingly quiet period and it also became apparent that promotion prospects for dog handlers were depressingly limited. So I went back to Malaya and got out of the dog section because it wasn't really happening, besides I was having a great time there. I was playing a lot of rugby for the Malacca Club – first-class rugby – and making a fool of myself doing virtually what I wanted.

Eventually they transferred me to the mortar platoon, otherwise known as the support platoon. This was where they put the bad boys – everybody who got into trouble was sent to the mortar platoon. But in some ways it was a promotion. It was smaller, more élite and, as opposed to a company of a hundred men, you were a platoon of maybe twenty. You had to be a little more competent to work their equipment than just to fire a rifle. A rifleman is just a rifleman, but if you're a support soldier you're a specialist. You're working with wombats or mobats or mortars. A mobat is a mounted recoilless rifle, 120mm, for shooting down tanks. The mortars we were working with were the brand new 81mm jobs, though unfortunately we only had three-inch ammo.

I went back to Borneo for the second time as a mortar-man, with a right flank mortar detachment. We fired a lot of rounds over there in support. We went on patrol a lot. There were a lot of incursions. The Indonesians would come over the border and attack our positions, trying to take back that part of Borneo which remained British. We lost some guys. Medals were won. A lot of shots were fired. Anyone who joins the Army must bargain with the idea of seeing shots fired in anger, though some people seem to spend their entire military lives trying to avoid action. I have to confess I rather enjoyed it.

We spent six months in a camp about the size of two football pitches called Serudong Loute. It was a heavily sandbagged outpost on one of the rivers separating the British-held northern part of the island from the rest of Borneo. Because of the danger of attack, the accommodation was all in underground dugouts and trenches and there wasn't much Rest and Recreation. One night, around Christmas, I went into the quartermaster's store and found this five-gallon jar of rum – army issue, black rum. I wasn't drinking alcohol at the time but I thought it might cheer up my friends so I took it out and gave it to everybody. Tucker Leach, our cook, ended up so drunk he fell out of his sentry post.

The authorities knew the rum had gone and they knew I'd taken it. They couldn't prove it however, so the sergeant major cancelled the nightly beer ration. No beer until the culprit was identified. I was sure I'd be bubbled before long but the company held out for three weeks. Beerless in Borneo for three weeks was no joke, I can tell you. Finally our Company Commander, Major Turner, told the sergeant major to restore the beer ration. He said he'd never known morale so high and he'd have been more disturbed if someone *had* given him my name.

One of the highpoints was the epic drama of the jetty on the River Loute. The base was re-supplied at regular intervals by hovercraft which didn't take long to skim upriver from our main base at the provincial town of Kuching. Trouble was the hovercraft was so noisy you could hear it coming for miles up this jungle river and the sound of its approach gave the local bandits plenty of time to get in position on the riverbank to take pot-shots at it. And it was so fast, streamlined and bumpy in the water that you couldn't really put a gun platform on the outside to give returning fire.

It was decided the mortar platoon would get the dirty job of building a jetty so the Royal Corps of Transport could come upriver in their little cargo ships which had Bren guns mounted fore and aft and were well able to look after themselves. We set about the task without too much enthusiasm, grumbling that we were sweating away just to make life easier for Transport crews who were scared of the odd bullet hole in their high-tech hovercraft toys. We hacked down timber in the jungle and dragged it through clearings to sink piles in the river mud and begin extending a line of planks out into the water. It was sweaty, back-breaking work and we were being urged on to greater and greater efforts by our platoon sergeant Ewan Laurie.

Sergeant Laurie is a remarkable man, a fine soldier who has now risen to the rank of Lieutenant Colonel and was recently awarded an MBE. He is now stationed in London at the Chelsea Pensioners' Hospital where he lovingly looks after the welfare of old soldiers. I learned a lot from Sergeant Laurie and not all of it was of a military nature. Ewan Laurie was a very moral man, not that he abstained from strong drink or anything like that, but he possessed great strength of character and great honesty.

At dawn every morning, Sergeant Laurie would appear on the river bank, his engineering plans in hand, and set the work schedule for the day. Every evening he would scrutinise the progress and pronounce himself satisfied or dissatisfied with the day's labours. He put his heart and soul into the project and the rest of us didn't really give a damn. In no time at all he had developed that maniacal glint in his eye and the sort of nervous energy that afflicted Alec Guinness in the movie *Bridge on the River Kwai*. We hadn't asked to build a jetty on the River Loute. We didn't want to build a jetty on the River Loute. But if our masters who held us captive in that stinking jungle forced us to do it, it would be the best damned jetty in all of South East Asia! Not quite in the same league as a multi-span rail bridge over a raging river gorge, but no mean feat for a bunch of mortarmen who had great difficulty solving those little construction puzzles you get on the backs of matchboxes.

Within weeks we were all caught up in Sergeant Laurie's infectious enthusiasm, giving it 'Colonel Bogey' as we whistled our way through the jungle with more timbers. The whole job took less than a month and when it was completed we all stood there, misty-eyed, chests swelling with that great orgasmic sense of accomplishment. I think there was even old soldiers' talk of having annual reunions at the Guards' depot in England on the anniversary of the jetty's completion, 'when all this hellish war is over and we can go back home'.

We stayed up late that night, not saying much, just admiring the slender, strong outline of the jetty glistening in the moonlight reflecting off the water. Sergeant Laurie sat off to one side, alone with his thoughts, bursting with pride at the magnificent monument thrusting out a good fifteen feet from the bank and soaring gracefully about four feet above water level. As a finishing touch, we slung a few old tyres on ropes at the end of the jetty, not to cushion the Transport boats, but to make sure they didn't damage our woodwork.

The following day was the opening ceremony when the first transport freighter pulled alongside and those heartless, unappreciative bastards casually threw drums of chemical lavatory disinfectants on to our virgin jetty. We lined up, lumps in throats, hands calloused, backs aching but stiff and erect, as if we were great harbourmasters welcoming the docking of the *Queen Elizabeth* for the first time. It really was impressive, but that night disaster struck. A sentry in the tower above the jetty woke the entire camp with a sustained burst of fire from a Bren gun. He was screaming, 'Enemy frogmen!'

We rolled out of bed and scrambled to our sandbagged fire positions. The mortar platoon, the proud jetty-builders, were prepared to kill mercilessly in defence of their beloved structure. As I went through the well-rehearsed drill of loading my ammunition, I paused for a moment and thought: Wait a minute. Indonesian frogmen? Fucking Indonesian frogmen?? It just didn't seem right. It didn't roll off the tongue. It was a military absurdity. It had the same ring to it as Eskimo paratroopers.

I stuck my head briefly above the sandbags. And then I saw them. Holy shit! Three of them, glistening in black wetsuits, crouching over the end of the jetty. We could hear the company sergeant major shouting at the sentry asking for fire directions. The mortar platoon braced themselves. A hundred yards to our left, No. 2 Platoon, who hadn't taken any part in the jetty-building project, didn't bother to wait for directions. They opened up with everything they had. The jetty was being ripped apart, planks flying up into the air and splintering as hundreds of high-velocity rounds crashed into them.

Eventually company headquarters managed to fire a two-inch flare dangling from a parachute above the jetty to shed some light on the subject. And we saw them quite clearly. Three, black, shiny, rubbery, very dead, Dunlop cross-ply tyres which we had put out as fenders. They had been pulled clear and stacked across the end of the jetty when the supply boat had left. Slowly one of them slipped off and was carried away by the current which was also sweeping away tons of bullet-riddled timber from the wreckage of the jetty. The hail of gunfire stopped abruptly. There was the sound of embarrassed tittering from No. 2 Platoon, then sporadic laughter, then outright derision and hilarity.

Sergeant Laurie clambered over the sandbags and stood in the clouds of gunsmoke. The light of the parachute flare was just dying away but you could see the disbelief and agony in his face. It reminded me of that scene in *Bridge on the River Kwai*, where Alec Guinness comes across William Holden on the river bed after Holden's just put explosive charges beneath the whole of Alec's precious bridge. Sergeant Laurie's face was just like that, only he wasn't acting. There was one near fatality that night: the sentry. Sergeant Laurie was going to strangle him with his bare hands.

We rebuilt the jetty. There was no complaining or moaning as we worked this time. Like the last time, No. 2 Platoon just looked on as we worked, nudging each other in the ribs, grinning and saying nothing. We got our revenge a couple of months later.

The camp was getting a visit from the Major General and the mortar platoon drew the short straw again. We were in charge of the unpleasant, but very necessary, task of camp hygiene. We had to ensure that drinking and washing water was sterilised and had to keep the chemical toilets serviced. Cleaning the chemlavs was done by emptying the lavatory bins into a dustbin, putting the dustbin into a wheelbarrow, wheeling the bins down to the assault boats, taking them downriver, and dumping the contents overboard. A sort of primitive version of modern British sewage treatment techniques.

Because of the General's visit that day, the latrine job had to be done earlier than normal, at breakfast-time. Breakfast was a big deal at the camp. The food wasn't bad. It usually consisted of fried bread, a couple of strips of fatty bacon, compo sausage and some beans. Quite tasty, there was just never very much of it. It was cooked in a field kitchen and served up in an open cookhouse which was just a flat area with a roof and laid out with benches.

As the rest of the company sat down to breakfast, myself and another mortarman came past on the pathway beside the cookhouse with a dustbin load of camp shit precariously balanced on our wheelbarrow. It was a job we had done countless times before, but this time, for some reason, we failed to take the turn off the plank running alongside the cookhouse, just where it led to the path to our re-built jetty. We slipped, the wheelbarrow wobbled, the dustbin full of shit slipped off, and a small tidal wave of excrement and chemicals went surging across the cookhouse floor.

All around us men were turning green and staggering off into the bush to retch and vomit. The rest of the mortar platoon then appeared for breakfast. They were tough men, veterans of camp hygiene duty. They were inured to smells which would reduce your average lavatory attendant to a choking, gasping wreck. They were the breed of men who built almost indestructible jetties. They sat down to the best breakfast they had ever enjoyed. Double, treble rations. As much bacon and beans and sausage as they could want. As small rivulets of chemical slime and shit eddied around their boots, they chomped on their fried bread and discussed the latest football results from back home, the incidence of venereal disease in Kuching brothels, the morality of warfare and the techniques of marine engineering, with specific reference to the construction of jetties and harbour installations.

Later that year, when we were posted back to Malaya, we went out and won the Major General's March and Shoot Competition. That competition was the most prestigious event of the year. You had to march ten miles with all your equipment, then have a shoot-off with self-loading rifles at a series of targets 100 yards away. You got inspected before you left and inspected at the end, so if you dumped any equipment you lost points. We finished at a run, and Danny White and I were carrying almost double the load – this one guy couldn't do it. Danny took his rifle, I took his pack, and we ran down to the finish line. We just blew the opposition away. The best platoon in the brigade. It was our way of saying thanks to Sergeant Ewan Laurie for teaching us how to maintain both appetite and dignity when the contents of the sewers back up into your breakfast cereal or when fate decrees that all your efforts are reduced to rubble and you have to start all over again.

Nobody thought we'd win because they thought we were just troublemakers. Danny White who wouldn't hestitate to shoulder the extra load for a comrade who just couldn't go on, was always getting put in the guardroom for fighting. I was just as bad. I once got twenty-one days detention for being absent without leave. It was a little matter of an exceedingly attractive nurse from the Women's Royal Army Corps I was dating in Singapore. She wouldn't let me go, so I was late home. If I'd been caught with her in bed or a bar I'd have been in even greater trouble but I managed to sneak back into camp without running foul of the military police. Then I gave myself up to the guardroom which was supposed to mitigate the offence. They still gave me twenty-one days, which was pretty stiff for a first offence. But they'd always wanted to catch me for something. In fact, I never did any of the time. The battalion rugby team was just off on tour and they were so desperate for me to play they cancelled the detention!

There was a great club in Malaya which was open to all members of our brigade – the 28th Commonwealth Infantry Brigade. It was just called the Beach Club and it was famous for its fights. They were spectacular, just like the brawls you see in the old westerns.

One I remember best was the time Danny White hit the Maori. We were all sitting at a table at the Club drinking and the Maoris were playing guitars and singing New Zealand songs. They're like the Welsh – they play great rugby and they sing beautifully. After a while they started passing the guitars around. Well, I can't play the guitar, so I passed it straight to Danny who couldn't play either, but he decided the polite thing was to have a bit of a strum. So after a bit of truly terrible noise, the head Maori, a great big bloke they called 'King', said, 'Hey, you Scottish motherfucker, pass the guitar on.' He said it in a perfectly playful, drunken way, but what he didn't realise was that there were two things you couldn't joke to Danny about: his mother and Scotland. And King had just done both.

So Danny says, 'What did you call me?' And the Maori grins and says it again.

I knew what would happen next, and sure enough Danny hit him. Danny was a big man, about six foot six, and it was a tremendous right hand which caught the big Maori square on the chin. It would have knocked out Mike Tyson or Marvin Hagler but the Maori never moved. Just sat there. Now Danny and I were the only two Scots Guards there, so I stood up alongside him and had a go myself. I hit him another thundering right hand, full on the chin. The guy just went on sitting there. Didn't move an inch. Only this time he let out a terrible roar. Danny and I just looked at each other and took off, ran straight out of the door of the Beach Club and down the street.

You have to know when you're beaten and when the two of you hit someone as hard as we hit the King and all he does is roar at you, then you know you're beaten and the only thing to do is get out fast. Poor Danny, he became quite a reformed character and rose to be Drill Sergeant but he was killed in the Falklands at the Battle of Tumbledown Mountain. We got into some terrible scrapes together but there was never anything bad about Danny. He was just a bit wild.

Another time we got mixed up with a couple of regiments in the 28th Commonwealth Infantry Brigade Group, the First New Zealand Regiment and the Third Royal Australian Regiment. And neither of them had really met British regiments before. Especially Scottish regiments. We and the Australians always seemed to be fighting and then the Irish Guards came out to join us and the situation went from bad to worse. First a couple of Irish Guardsmen got beaten up in one of the little bars just outside the camp gates, then some Australians got beaten up, then some more Irish Guards. So one night we decided we would go over to the Australian lines and sort them out once and for all.

Almost the entire battalion put on boots and puttees and denims, armed themselves with any weapon they could find and raced across the football field, which was all that separated us from the Aussies. There were no windows in their huts because of the heat, so we just climbed straight in. My friend Spike Lawson and a couple of guys from left flank broke into their orderly room and stole their colours. They didn't like that.

It ended with both regiments on the rugby field facing each other in underwear and pyjamas. The two sergeants majors actually came to blows. The Irish Guards on standby patrol were called out with fixed bayonets to keep us apart. After that the Major General in charge of the Commonwealth Brigade wouldn't allow both regiments to go out on the town on the same night. The Aussies could go out Mondays, Wednesdays and Fridays, and we'd go out Tuesdays, Thursdays and Saturdays.

I'm afraid I was in very little danger of promotion in Malaya. Then in 1967, we got posted back to Edinburgh Castle to do guard duty there. Two hours on and four off for twenty-four hours. It was what I'd been doing two years before, only Edinburgh was colder and less exciting than London. I didn't want to be that sort of ceremonial toy soldier again. It was a traumatic change for me after wearing combat gear all day with jungle boots and jungle hat to wear tunics and bearskins once more and walk up and down outside the castle!

The Grand National was being run then. I never bet on racehorses and don't really know anything about them. But this guy said, 'Do you want a bet in the National? I'll put one on for you,' and I said, 'Yeah, might as well. I'll put three quid on it.'

So he came back and said, 'I picked a horse.'

I said, 'What's the horse's name?'

And he said, 'Foinavon.'

It meant nothing to me. 'What price is it?'

'100 to 1,' he said.

I didn't even watch the race. The odds were ridiculous. It obviously didn't have a chance and I went out with Norrie for a drink instead. Then we got back to the barracks and heard there'd been this incredible tumble at Becher's Brook. Almost all the horses fell but Foinavon was so far back it was clear of all the trouble. It wove its way through all the debris of prostrate horses and injured jockeys and won the race.

Suddenly I had two hundred pounds in my hand. You can buy yourself out of the Army with that, I thought. Time to try Civvy Street. So I did.

Guyana

It was a jolt at first. I went to Jersey in the Channel Islands in the beginning and worked as a builder's labourer humping bricks around. Nice enough place – the booze is cheap and because it's a holiday island the night-life is O K. Always girls looking for a good time. After all those years of discipline and orders it was a relief to be my own boss. Labouring in the open air at least kept me in reasonable physical shape, but it didn't exactly present a challenge and in due course I started to get restless.

For a while I went back to Scotland where I found a job at Rolls-Royce, in the Time and Motion department. More time than motion as far as I was concerned. I was on the night shift, measuring times on a slide rule and telling people they should've made fifty more articles in the last twenty-five minutes. I really couldn't handle that, so pretty soon I quit the job. My mother knew the provost of Motherwell, the equivalent of mayor, and she fixed me a job offer as a policeman. A policeman in Motherwell! That didn't sound much more exciting than the Time and Motion department. Of course had I known then what I know now about the perks and fiddles open to policemen, I might just have been tempted to join them and take a lot of money in my back pocket. But I didn't know and I didn't join. I was just at a loose end and desperately hoping something would turn up. Which is why I landed up in South America.

Guyana used to be British Guiana, and it's between Venezuela and Surinam, or Dutch Guiana, and Brazil. It's coastal in the north, becomes very mountainous inland with heavy forests, and is then more or less grassland over the Tagatu mountains down towards Brazil. It has very little importance in the scheme of things. It's been basically communist since it became independent from Britain in the sixties. The language spoken there is either Portuguese or Wopishana, a local Indian dialect, or a mixture of the two. The name 'Guyana' means 'land of many waters'.

I'd been out of the Army for a couple of years. I was twenty-four years old and I was frittering my life away. My mother was constantly worrying about me and always combing the small ads columns in the newspapers, hoping she'd find me a nice job. One day she saw an advertisement in a Scottish farming weekly. It had been placed by a man called Jimmy Brown, who was the maintenance manager for a ranch in South America called Dadanawa. It said: 'Young man wanted as assistant ranch manager. Must be able to ride a horse and be a strong swimmer. Must also be used to tropical climates.' She said: 'John, here's a wonderful opportunity for you.'

I really wasn't that interested, but I liked to humour her so I sent off an application. A few days later I got this letter back from a holding company in England and they invited me to go to the Caledonian Hotel in Edinburgh for an interview.

At that time it was one of the best hotels in Edinburgh, very old-fashioned, very formal. So I dressed myself up in my best Sunday suit – brigade tie and all – and drove the fifty-odd miles to the city prepared to put on the style. I wasn't the only candidate. There were quite a lot of people being interviewed. I hadn't been expecting that and I found myself getting quite nervous till eventually my turn came and I went in to see two men: a Major

Betancourt-Gomez, and a Mr Turner. Turner was the previous manager of the ranch and he seemed all right; Betancourt-Gomez turned out to be a major in the Guyana Defence Force and he didn't seem quite so all right. The name was a bit of a no-no for a start, though I suppose that wasn't his fault.

They explained that the present manager of the ranch was retiring and they were looking for a replacement. The guy who was retiring was actually quite famous. His name was Stan Brock, and he found fame on an American TV series called 'Wildlife Kingdom', sponsored by the Mutual of Omaha insurance company. He'd been on the ranch for years and years and his speciality was catching exotic animals which he trained to do extraordinary things. He came to Britain and went on TV with a harpie eagle. He had wrestled anacondas. He was an unusual sort of person. He'd left in a hurry to take up a position in America, working with a wildlife film company, and that left the job open.

It was said to be the largest ranch in the world at that time – 2 million acres, 2,000 square miles. It ran 40,000 head of cattle – crossbred Sanagatruzis, Brahmins, Charolais, all sorts of weird concoctions – and about five or six thousand head of horse. There was also a lot of wildlife to contend with – ocelots, tapirs, mountain-lions, monkeys, gibbons, pigs.

I told them I'd lived on a farm and could ride a horse and swim. Betancourt-Gomez asked if I'd been in the military, and seemed impressed to hear that I'd been in the Scots Guards. I could imagine what his military experience was: organising five or six barefoot peasants to put out brush fires and chase stray cattle. In Britain he'd have been lucky to get a commission in the Catering Corps.

They told me more about the ranch. They said it was a very isolated place – 400 miles from the nearest town. I liked the idea. Ever since Africa I'd loved being off in the bush on my own. And it certainly beat Time and Motion or the Motherwell Police. South America sounded like *Rawhide* and here I was, Rowdy Yates, going out to rope and ride. Also I was engaged to be married and this sounded like a great place to avoid temptation. It didn't sound as if there was a lot of night-life down on the ranch.

The interview lasted about forty minutes. They told me to wait downstairs, and then the two of them came down to the lobby and said to all of us, 'We'd like to invite you to come for a swim.' That got rid of a couple of the candidates right there. They just made their excuses and left. God alone knows why they'd answered the ad in the first place. Perhaps they thought they'd walk on water if they were thrown in at the deep end. They ushered the remaining fifteen of us into a bus and took us to Portobello, which is a seaside town about twenty miles away. On the way out, the guy I was sitting next to said, 'Do you think they're gonna make us ride too? I've never been on a horse in my life. I thought I'd have a lot of time to practise once I got there.'

They'd obviously rented the pool for the occasion – there was nobody else around. They gave us each a pair of overalls and told us to swim two lengths of the pool and then tread water. At the time, the whole thing seemed very strange, but, in retrospect, I can understand it. Why take somebody's word that he can swim, ship him 5,000 miles to South America, and the first time they've got to drive cattle across the river he drowns? It's worse than embarrassing, it's inconvenient.

I'm not the world's most stylish swimmer. But I can thrash along. And I'm a very good floater. In the Army they teach you to use your clothes as a flotation device, by taking them off, tying the arms and legs closed tight, throwing them over your head and catching air in them. A pair of overalls hold air in anyway, if you button them up to the neck, and I'd tucked my cuffs into my socks. The

ones who'd lied about being able to swim – six or seven –
were excused from the next part of the interview, which
was conducted at a riding stable in Ingliston. They put us
all on horses and asked us to walk, trot and canter our
mounts. That eliminated all but five or six of us. And that
was that.

Three weeks later I got another letter from the holding
company, asking me to have a chest X-ray and send them
the results. It was a dusty climate, and they wanted to
make sure I had no chest problems. About three weeks
after that I got a contract through the mail offering me a
position as assistant ranch manager. I'd get a month's
paid holiday every two years, and a week's holiday, to be
spent locally, every three months. Why me? Some of the
others were too young, some were too old, but I think
Betancourt-Gomez probably had a lot to do with the
selection, and my military background was probably
what did the trick: Brigade of Guards, stiff upper lip,
takes orders well.

I travelled out to Georgetown, the Guyana capital, spent a
quiet weekend there and then flew down to the ranch on
Monday. The airport there was pretty basic, a single east-
west runway and a tin shack with a Pepsi machine in the
corner. I flew in a twin-engined Dakota with no seats, just
provisions and machinery for the ranch, all lashed to the
floor. The only other passengers were a goat and six
chickens. The pilot was a big fat guy in shorts who looked
as if he'd been given the boot by Pan Am for doing cocaine
or screwing cabin crew. That's the sort of pilot you get
flying Dakotas in South America. The catering was on the
same level too – a couple of curled sandwiches in a brown
paper bag.

Three hours later the fat pilot opened the door and
called out, 'Landing in five minutes.' I looked out of the
window – no sign of civilisation. We bumped down this

field and a Land-Rover rolled up out of nowhere. The driver was a guy of around sixty, with a weatherbeaten face, shock of white hair and hands like pigskin.

'You must be the new assistant manager,' he said. 'I'm Jimmy Brown.' And that was it. He was the maintenance manager who'd put the ad in the paper. I later discovered he was the world's most silent human. Never spoke unless he had to, and then only in moderation. The only time he got really talkative was when one of the locals irritated him. Then he'd kick them in the arse and swear in Wopishana.

We drove about half a mile down a dry riverbed, through a single gate and there inside the fence was a big white painted house on stilts. The stilts, I learned later, were to keep the termites away. There were three or four bedrooms and a kitchen sunk in a cellar to keep it cool. The living room had a nice colonial balcony and cowskin chairs with arms so long you could put your legs up on them, and the arms had little holes for glasses. Everything was made out of animal skin and wood.

I was assigned to a room with mosquito nets which I was extremely careful to pull over me at night on account of the vampire bats – they carried rabies. It was difficult to sleep beside the old whirring fan, powered from a noisy gasoline generator, but it was home sweet home, and it made a change from the barracks.

Across the way was Jimmy Brown's house, a little bungalow on stilts. And behind the main house was the help's house where the maid and three other guys lived. If you looked from my veranda over to the right, there was a bunkhouse where the *vaqueros* or herdsmen lived. They were Amerindian-Wopishana natives. Behind that were corrals for the horses and barns where the vehicles were kept.

Only five or six buildings in the middle of two million acres! When the *vaqueros* were gone the place was kind of deserted. They used to round up cattle there four times a year, and because of the size of the property, they had different round-up stations, each one with a little house. You'd move there, and stay for three or four days, round up the cattle in that area, then move on to the next round-up area.

Mr Turner, the old guy who had interviewed me in Edinburgh along with the Guyanese 'Catering Corps' major, had been re-activated after Stan Brock's abrupt departure. He was going to be there for three months while I learned the ropes and then I was going to be the ranch manager. Turner introduced me to Jerome Marx, who was the *vaquero* foreman, and the cook, whose name was Mary. Jerome spoke a bit of English, but he had a funny way with the language. Mary's English was a shade better.

They found me a horse named Red, which had been Stan Brock's mount. It took them a couple of days to track it down, and it hadn't been ridden for a year. Terrific! Horses were vital and the only reliable way of covering the territory. Jimmy Brown tried to keep all the running stock moving on the ranch: three or four ex-military Land-rovers, a swamp buggy with big balloon wheels, a couple of trucks with flatbed trailers, but the vehicles couldn't get very far because of all the water around there.

Red was at least a reasonable size – bigger than most of the other horses – but the saddles were smaller than either American or English saddles, with no saddlehorn. They made me a lasso out of plaited hide – about four feet of it would stick straight out before it would bend – that was tied on to the saddle girth, and they told me we were going to go round up. 'Oh, great,' I said.

We were all ready the next day, a tractor was there with all the food, like a chuck wagon, and we started to ride off. These Savannah ponies go at a really uncomfortable jog trot – they don't canter, they don't walk. You just sit there being shaken about. I said, 'Where's the round-up station?' And they said: 'D'you see those hills there? Right on the horizon? It's about a day's ride over them.' 'Oh fuck!' I said.

It took us three days to ride to this round-up station. By that time my arse was so sore you wouldn't believe it. I hadn't ridden for months and months, and now I was spending seven hours a day on a horse. Every muscle in my body was in abject shock and protest. We slept in hammocks which I never could manage but at least it was reasonably comfortable for the backside.

The *vaqueros* were all waiting for me to fall off the horse. They wanted to see what I was all about. I used to go at night and drink casaba wine with them. The hooch was distilled from the casaba plant and was milky white and exceedingly potent. The first night out there they said: 'Do you like meat?'

I said, 'Yeah.'

They said, 'Do you like fillet?'

I said, 'Oh, yeah.'

They said, 'We'll go get you some.'

The nearest butcher must have been several hundred miles away, so I was a bit surprised. I should have realised. Out they went and roped a calf, dragged it in, cut its throat, opened it up, cut the fillet out, and gave it to me. They gave me the best bit and took the rest themselves. One day I saw Jerome take the ovaries out of a cow. Just cut into the flank, stuck his hand in, grabbed the ovaries out, threw them away, and covered the wound with some sort of bitumen. The cow just wandered off.

When we got to the round-up station, we rounded all these cows up and put them in a corral. We'd put them through a narrow wooden alleyway called a race and count them. At the end of the race, there were two gates into two other corrals. They'd put clean-skins, calves that hadn't been branded before, into one corral. You had to

44

brand them and castrate the bulls. As the previous round-up would have been a year before, some of these bulls were quite well developed. Like any self-respecting male they objected to having their balls cut off and they made a bit of a fuss about it. So there was usually some excitement.

The *vaqueros*, maybe twenty of them plus the foreman, got up at four in the morning to go out and round up. I didn't go with them. They used to give me coffee to drink that was like instant adrenalin: thick, black, dirty coffee. They used to grind the beans with a mortar and pestle. They never let anybody drink the stuff after midday. If you did, you'd never get to sleep. You went to bed when it got dark, because there wasn't anything else to do. It's not like the movies with everybody sitting around the chuck wagon singing cowboy songs by the fireside. They'd just sling the hammocks, hobble the horses and turn in.

As assistant manager my basic job was to keep the books. I had to count how many calves had been born since the last round-up, how many cows branded, how many bulls, how many cattle sold, and where they were shipped. The foreman's job was to organise the round-up, but the manager took responsibility for it.

It was hilly, undulating ground like the pampas. A lot of high grass, but not great grass. Never green. The cattle weren't very healthy looking, unlike European stock raised on superior grazing, and they were also at risk from cheetahs and wild pigs. Every cow needed three acres of that land to graze on, so they did a lot of walking.

The two people who started cattle ranching down there were an American called Hart and a Scot called Melville. Originally they used to drive cattle 600 miles to the coast and ship them for sale to Louisiana. They were real pioneers. They had married local Wopishana women, and their kids were half Guyanese. They ran this whole area. They'd built schools and a mission and they loved the people there. They were the sole employers; if you worked at all, you worked for the Harts or the Melvilles. When Britain gave Guyana its independence from British Guiana, the new Nationalist Prime Minister, Forbes Burnham, and his mob, said to these people, 'You've got two years to wind up your businesses and get out of the country.'

Burnham obviously thought the Harts and the Melvilles were a threat. They were 400 miles away from his capital in Georgetown and they just kept on running things their own way. I don't think Burnham liked that. So he opened up an administrative centre at Lethem, the provincial capital for that part of the country, with soldiers and a local government official stationed there. Our ranch, of course, was run by the Guyanese, so there was no trouble.

Eventually Guyana became communist. Burnham was Moscow-educated, a hard-core Marxist, and under him the country was devastated. So the Harts and the Melvilles didn't care for Mr Burnham any more than he cared for them. No one I spoke to in Guyana liked Burnham. They preferred being governed by the British empire. They couldn't wait to get rid of British rule, but they'd give anything to have it back.

For years there had been a border dispute between Guyana and Venezuela. The river dividing them had changed its course, which not surprisingly had complicated matters. When Hart and Melville were told they had to get out of Guyana, Venezuela came to them and said, 'Listen, don't go. Hang in there, stage a coup, declare yourself an independent republic. We can't intervene without that, because it would be an act of aggression against the sovereign state of Guyana. But if you declare an independent republic and ask for help then we're coming to the assistance of a people's liberation movement and everyone will love us.' So they sent over a whole lot of weapons as a goodwill gesture.

About five days after that first round-up we got back to base and the Harts and the Melvilles came over for a drink. They were our nearest neighbours even though they were five or six hours' drive away. It seemed a neighbourly thing to do but I soon realised they'd come to suss me out. Over the casaba wine they told me their story. I was very sympathetic. Their entire life's work was about to be destroyed by Burnham's expulsion order. When they'd finished they asked me what I had done before coming to Guyana. 'Brigade of Guards,' I said.

'Oh, really?' they said. 'We've got all these weapons and we don't know what to do with them. Do you know anything about weapons?'

'A little,' I said. 'What've you got?'

'Oh, some mortars and rocket launchers.' And they invited me to come and visit them.

I met them at Hart's place; both Melville and Hart were there. It was just another ranch. A couple of wooden houses on stilts, painted white. Very simple. The weapons they were talking about were hidden in a dried-up river bed, covered with a tarpaulin, stashed under a pile of brush. They had no idea what they were all about – these guys were farmers. What they had was an 81mm mortar with C2 sights. The 81mm round is quite complicated. There's a primary charge and seven variants, each one closely related to the angle of depression of the barrel which determines where they will all land. You don't just put a bomb down a tube like they do in the movies. They also had 3.5-inch rocket launchers and general-purpose machine-guns. All were sophisticated ex-British Army items.

The ammunition was green-spot, which was good. The spots tell the age of the ammunition, how long it's been around. The British Army won't use ammunition over a certain age, they'll give it to other people who aren't so choosy. Since Guyana was once British, they would say,

'There's 14 million rounds we never used last month; not safe any longer, let's give it to the Guyanese.' They were just being ultra-cautious. Most of this stuff was good, probably just as good as anything being used in Britain at that time.

So I saw this impressive little arsenal and I said, 'Do your guys, your *vaqueros*, know how to work this stuff?'

'Not a clue,' Hart said. 'Do you?'

I explained I'd spent most of my adult life with these things.

'Well, could you teach them?'

I didn't know what to think. Here I was in the middle of South America, being asked to command a revolutionary army. I was going to be Che Guevara – a full colonel at least, maybe a general. It's something I really enjoy doing, the military thing, and tactics. I'd be in command for the first time of my own little force. It would be a small, self-contained unit, Jerome would be my sergeant-major and I trusted Jerome. But, hell, these were just kids of nineteen or twenty. They roped, they branded, they ate rice, they squatted down in the fields to shit, and they didn't speak English.

Finally they said, 'John, would you be prepared to throw your lot in with us completely?'

It must have been the casaba wine because I said yes. I could say that I felt a tug at my heartstrings. I could tell you I acted from the purest motives, that I was determined to save these wretched people from Marxist dictatorship, that I had a passionate need to fight for democracy and freedom. But the truth was that I was getting to do something a little more exciting than watching bulls getting their balls cut off, I was getting to be a soldier again. I mean who really cared about Hart and Melville? Who gave a monkey's toss about Forbes Burnham? But leading a revolution? That was something else.

So I said, 'What exactly do you want to do?' If they

wanted to storm Georgetown, they didn't have enough weapons or men. But if they wanted to heat up the administration centre, they had plenty.

They said, 'We want to take over the administration centre and form an independent republic.' And then Hart said something I'll never forget as long as I live 'John,' he said, 'when this is over there'll be a place for you in the government, when it's formed.'

Oh well, I thought, if not Dictator, at least I can be Minister of Defence: fly-pasts, uniform with scrambled egg on the cap, motorcycle escorts, beautiful mistresses . . . 'No problem,' I said.

Now the administration centre, as I said, was in Lethem. A small building from which the local government administered the area. It had about twenty-five or thirty soldiers who used to go out on a regular basis and show a presence. There was a short-wave radio to communicate with Georgetown, and a couple of little houses where the people lived who worked in and around the administration centre. It also had an airstrip, which was really just a field.

We went back to the Harts' house and decided on a plan. There was me, and Hart and Melville – both men of about sixty-five to seventy – Mrs Hart, two of Melville's boys and three of Hart's boys. The sons ranged in age from twenty-five to thirty. They had it all worked out: Mrs Hart was going to be President of the Republic which was to be named Rupinninny. They had even designed a flag.

I had to inject a little realism, so I told them in my opinion what would happen. Obviously there were regular radio calls placed to Georgetown from the administration centre. That's standard operating procedure anywhere. Any military organisation has a fixed schedule of times when headquarters and bases make contact. I said, 'If you take this administration centre over, you're going to have to be prepared to kill people.

The guys in the administration centre are bound to radio Georgetown and tell them what's happening.'

And they said, 'Yes, we understand that.'

'So,' I said, 'once you've taken over and made Mrs Hart President, what's the plan then? Because I'm going to tell you what the Government are going to do. They'll be prepared to kill people too.'

They said, 'Yeah, but we're going to knock out the airstrip so they can't land.'

I said, 'Well, they have these things now called parachutes. And they'll put them on and jump out of the planes without needing to land them and they'll come and kick your arses.'

They said, 'We don't care. We want to do this.'

They showed me a map of the area where all the airstrips were. At least we could put them out of commission. Put down oil drums, trees, anything we could lay our hands on. Then, I said, we'd attack the administration centre, take it over and install Mrs Hart as President. 'At that point,' I said, 'you talk to your people in Venezuela. Tell them you're a republic, tell them Mrs Hart's the President, and tell them to get up here immediately. Because if you don't, the Guyana Defence Force are gonna be down here within the week. If they don't have airborne capabilities they'll drive in. Maybe even march. But they'll be here, for sure, sooner or later.'

They said, 'Yeah, we know that.'

I said, 'You've not got the remotest possibility of containing them on your own. You've no chance in the world. No matter how bad the Guyana Defence Force are, your mob's worse. So the Venezuelans have got to be here. They're the only people who can help you. Can you trust these people?'

'Well,' they said, 'they sent us the guns.'

I said, 'Fair enough. We attack the admin. centre.'

And I began to make plans, one of which was a private

arrangement between Jerome and me that we would have horses ready so that if the Venezuelans didn't arrive to support us, we'd be off to Brazil and the Harts and the Melvilles could sort the problem out on their own. That may sound a little ungallant, but I was only being realistic. If the Venezuelans didn't arrive within hours of our uprising, the Guyanese Army would kill the lot of us. A good general always has a plan of retreat.

There wasn't time to go back to the ranch where all my gear was. The Harts and the Melvilles had been arguing with Burnham for over a year. They'd been told to get out, and they'd been bullshitting around, and now there was only so much time to get this accomplished. Not only that, the longer we stayed down there getting these *vaqueros* ready, the more chance there was of somebody getting back to Georgetown and saying, 'There's a guy down there from the Scots Guards shooting rockets around and firing weapons.' People can hear high-velocity weapons from miles away, and the administration centre wasn't that far off. So I said, 'Go for it, let's do it.'

I spent the next three days trying to teach these *vaqueros* how to use weapons. All of them had rifles – prehistoric muzzle loaders – because there were a lot of wild animals about. And they all had this natural instinctive ability to shoot, and shoot very well. But it's something else trying to tell somebody how to fire a thousand rounds a minute as you change a barrel on a general-purpose machine-gun, while watching that the belt doesn't expend itself. And how to load a 3.5-inch rocket. And fire a mortar. These are things it takes six months to teach a trained soldier who speaks English. I was trying to teach a handful of Wopishana-speaking *vaqueros* in a couple of days. A tall order. Still, all we were going to do was take the admin. centre which was only manned by a platoon of goons anyway. Then the Venezuelans would come and take over and all we had to do was form a government. No problem.

51

We picked up the equipment and took it to within a couple of miles of Lethem. Then at 4 a.m. we drove to within 200 yards of the admin. centre – the biggest building in town, seven or eight rooms, adobe built.

My most sensible guy carried the 3.5-inch rocket launcher. It was electronically detonated. You have to put the projectile in the back and hook two wires up, then ignite it by battery. He was quite sensible but I couldn't trust him to load, close the Venturi, hook up the wires and get out of the way of the backblast. The backblast would have barbecued anyone in the way. So I loaded the rockets and said, 'Just fire them. When they're gone, they're gone. When you've finished, put it down and forget about it.' Same with the machine-guns. I put some belts together so they wouldn't have to fiddle around changing them. All they had to do was aim and pull the trigger.

None of it was easy. I don't even speak enough Wopishana to say 'shut up', so I couldn't explain to the guy how to aim properly. These rockets are meant to hit tanks, right? So I just took the rocket launcher and aimed it in the direction of the admin. building for him. And I told him not to change anything. But, of course, the second my back was turned the bastard moved it. Every time I looked away he changed something.

Dawn was breaking. The guys in the admin. centre didn't suspect a thing. All fast asleep. Not a sound. After a few minutes when everything was set, I shouted, 'Fire!' The first round screamed right over the building. It missed the radio antenna and headed off in the general direction of Brazil. The result of this was that the guy over-corrected and the next round slammed into the earth about fifty yards in front of us. Dust and rocks all over the place! By this time any idea of a surprise attack had vanished. The noise was stupendous. I was screaming, 'Fire those fucking machine-guns for Chrissake!' The windows of the administration building started to open. The soldiers inside may have been dopey but even they realised something fairly serious was going on out there. So they started shooting back.

To be honest, once the actual shit hit the fan, my guys were good. They were shooting well. They were shooting accurately. They were going to get killed themselves if they didn't, so there was an incentive there. Besides which the enemy were frankly pretty dreadful. They shot wildly and they made easy targets. It was only a few minutes before the firing stopped from their side and a white night shirt was poked out of a window on the end of a stick.

So, we had taken the administration centre. Myself, the two Hart boys, one of the Melvilles' boys and Jerome were the first people in. The final total given in the newspapers was twenty-seven soldiers and policemen killed. We went in, took over the radio and told Melville and Hart what had happened. Mrs Hart was driven to the administration centre and sworn in. The survivors seemed quite pleased at the idea of her being President instead of Forbes Burnham but I was already busy looking at my watch. The Venezuelans were late.

There was a little celebration, no booze or anything, but people were happy. Some were looking at the bodies, some were trying to take the dead out. The building was like a bank after a raid by Butch Cassidy and the Sundance Kid, bullet holes all over the adobe.

Still nothing from Venezuela.

I said to the Melvilles and the Harts, 'I want all these people laid out, so that when the Guyana Defence Force comes down here, or the Venezuelans arrive, you can identify them.' I was making people take the names down, making sure all the corpses were identified, trying to be at least a little civilised about the whole thing. They were people's sons or husbands or whatever, relatives who

53

should be told when there are casualties. So we had them all laid out, covered with tarpaulins. The wounded were being treated as best we could, and they were put in a secure area too. Still no Venezuelans. And it was 4 p.m.

No communications had come through from Lethem to Georgetown, so the Government must have been starting to worry. A twin-engined plane flew over, couldn't land because all the airstrips had been doctored, and disappeared. I said to Mr Hart and Mr Melville, 'No Venezuelans!'

And then I said, 'Listen, I've made my position clear. Without outside help this operation is doomed. I'm awfully sorry about it but I said that all along. I promised to help but I didn't promise to die for you. No Venezuelans, no me. I'm gonna disappear. Any minute now there's gonna be people coming here wondering what the hell's going on. And there is no way in the world that this mob here can do anything about the Guyana Defence Force. So if the Venezuelans aren't here by five o'clock, I'm gone.'

They said, 'We understand, and thank you very much for all your help.'

I asked what they were going to do and they said, 'Well, nothing. This is our home.'

I felt bad, but what was I supposed to do? My home was in Motherwell. The Majestic ballroom and the Time and Motion department of Rolls-Royce were suddenly calling me. So Jerome and I got on our horses and rode off into the sunset. Just like in the movies. We went across the nearest border to Brazil, to a place called Boa Vista and got some accommodation there. For the next two weeks we would go back over the border to our round-up station, round up cattle and take them back to Boa Vista to sell. That's how we were getting money. The Guyana Defence Force, meanwhile, went bananas. Melville and Hart and his wife all got arrested. For all I know they're dead or they're still in jail. The sons were killed in a gun battle, though I think one was executed after he was taken to prison. We'd keep coming back over the border, nicking cattle, and we'd hear gossip about what was going on from local people.

Since I'd been out of the country for nearly a month, I decided that it was time I went back to Dadawana to see if there was any mail for me, and to get my gear. Everything I owned was still at the ranch because I'd never returned there after the uprising. Jerome and I rode back to the house, picked up some stuff, and as I was coming out a twin-engined plane landed. Four or five people got out. They were armed and they were looking for me.

If I had thought there was any way to get away, I would have done it. But what do you do, jump on a horse and get chased by a plane? Then guys showed up in Land-rovers. They all had weapons. It was really quite flattering. I got in the vehicle and they drove me to Lethem. In Lethem they put me in a plane and flew me to Georgetown. In Georgetown, they put me in jail.

The first jail was called Brick Dam Prison, but I was only there four hours. Then they moved me to Ivalleria, which is a Special Branch prison. A sort of Guyanese Lubianka. I was all on my own. Jerome had managed to get away, I'm not sure how. I guess they weren't too worried about him. I was the guy they wanted – a bloody foreign mercenary coming to their country and fomenting revolution. I guessed Forbes Burnham and his mates would be out for my blood.

As soon as I got to Ivalleria I was taken up to an office where the Chief Superintendent began to question me. It was dead spooky. He had all my military records, knew where I'd served, what I'd done, when I'd come into the country, the whole thing. I kept denying I'd been involved in the revolt. 'Can't think what you're talking about, Officer. I'm a British subject. I insist on seeing the Ambassador. I've been in a round-up station. Lethem? Never heard of it. Twenty-seven corpses? Good heavens, how perfectly dreadful, but you Latin Americans have a reputation for that sort of thing, don't you?'

I tell you I tried everything but the one thing that I wasn't going to do was to admit to anything at all. That's fatal. Doesn't matter how guilty you are, smile sweetly and deny everything. He'd only got the Harts' and the Melvilles' word for it, and I was certainly going to dispute that. 'Lying bastards! They are trying to frame me!'

I thought I put up a brilliant performance, but the Guyanese secret police didn't seem too impressed. They led me off to a little compound with two cells, put me in the far cell and locked the door of that and of the compound, too. They obviously thought they'd caught a real Houdini.

It was very dull in solitary. They took me out twice a day to exercise. I got to walk around the compound which was about forty by twenty metres and they put me back in the cell with garbage to eat: rice and fish-heads. I used to say, 'What time is it? Have you got a newspaper? What's the cricket score?' No dice. They were as silent as Jimmy Brown back on the ranch. After four or five days, the jailer came in again. I said, same as usual, 'What time is it, by the way?'

This time, instead of ignoring me, he says, 'Two o'clock. What do you want to eat?'

I said, 'What do you mean, what do I want to eat?' He had me worried for once, so I was stalling.

He said, 'Do you want anything special to eat?'

They do this in interrogation, of course. Standard procedure. You build people up and you bring them down, build them up and bring them down. It disorients them, weakens their resistance. It's basic army training and I knew the routine backwards. It's an accepted way of doing things. So I thought, OK, sunshine, if that's the way you want it, that's the way you get it, and I said, 'I'd like a fillet steak, medium rare, creamed potatoes, green peas, fresh fruit, and a pint of malted milk. Oh, and a newspaper and some magazines: *Time, Life* . . .' And he nodded politely and says, 'OK.'

It's true he didn't ask if I wanted French or English mustard and he didn't offer béarnaise sauce. OK, so he hadn't been trained at the Ritz and he wasn't the world's greatest maître d'. Never mind, the guy was doing his best. So I laughed. What else could I do? The normal thing that happens is you sit and wait for the food to come, they bring you the rice and fish-heads and you go, 'Aw, fuck.' So I thought, rice and fish-heads coming up. No big deal, no disappointment. Pretty soon, however, there was a steak, mashed potatoes, green peas, malted milk, papers . . . It was good steak, but the peas were a bit mushy.

I finished the meal and the guard came in and said, 'The superintendent wants to see you now.' So I'm taken down to this guy's office. There's a guy on my right with a machine-gun, the guy on my left's got a gun in a holster. And suddenly I begin to get bad feelings. They'd brought me a decent meal and papers, just as I'd asked. Jesus, I thought, maybe I'm a condemned man and they've been granting me my last wish!

First thing the super asks is my name.

'Come on,' I said. 'You know my name.' I said it with a lot of bravado, but I wasn't feeling too good. It was bizarre. It was all on his files. Parents' names. Religion. Place of birth. He even asked my age: 'Are you twenty-four years old?'

I'd never given it much thought before but suddenly it felt awful young. 'Yeah,' I said. 'Twenty-four and never been kissed.' Well, I thought, if you're going to die, you'd better die like a true Brit with a quip on your lips and a smile in your eyes.

So he finally says, 'It's my duty to inform you that you'll be taken from here at zero-seven-thirty hours tomorrow . . .' I never even heard the rest. I didn't need to. It was too bloody obvious, I'd read it in dozens of crime novels, seen it on the silver screen more times than I can remember. You know how it goes: '. . . taken to a place of execution . . .' I'd be hanged by the neck until dead. I thought of those movies where the guy is about to get shot and they ask him if he wants a blindfold and he says, 'No, thanks awfully.'

'Cigarette?'

'Yes, I think I will have a cigarette.' And he stands at this post, smiling sardonically and blowing perfect smoke rings while nine gorillas pump lead into him. I thought, 'There's no way in the world I would do that.' I'd be screaming and biting people. So while the superintendent is pronouncing sentence I'm just thinking, 'If I whack this guy on the right hand side of me, I'll grab his gun and shoot as many of them as I can.' At least I'd have the satisfaction of taking some of the bastards with me.

I was about to hit the guy on the right when I said absentmindedly, 'What did you say . . .?' And the superintendent said it again, in a bored monotone. 'That's right. We're deporting you. You leave for the airport at seven-thirty hours. We trust you have enjoyed your stay.'

The next morning the British consul, who hadn't been anywhere near me, met me at the airport. He was a typical failed diplomat, all blah and no chin. Obviously they'd said, 'Where can we send this guy where he won't cause any problems?' And somebody answered, 'Guyana, nothing ever happens there.' So he turns up in a crumpled tropical suit and he says, 'I'm so terribly pleased to see that you're all right. Were you treated well?'

I said, 'Yeah. Why didn't you come to see me?'

He said, 'They wouldn't let me.'

'What do you mean they wouldn't let you?' I said. 'I'm a British subject. You should have threatened them with a bloody gunboat.'

He said, 'We have to work with these people all the time and we don't want to upset them.'

So I thought, great! I'm banged up for a week, maybe facing a firing squad, and he doesn't want to come to see me because he doesn't want to upset anybody. No wonder the Empire's gone down the drain.

The plane landed en route from Rio to New York. I got on. I had ten days' growth of beard and I stank. I had a shirt, hat, jeans, pair of boots – nothing else. It was February, it was snowing at Kennedy when I arrived. They took my passport and gave it to the purser who came up and asked if I'd like a drink. They'd obviously been told, 'This guy's getting deported. Here's his passport and don't let him off anywhere.'

So the purser said, 'The drink's on us.'

I said, 'I'd love a beer.'

He brought me a Carlsberg Special, really strong. Best drink of my life. I had another. And another. By the time we were out over the Atlantic I was feeling pleasantly pissed. Close shave, I thought. Though a close shave was one thing I wasn't having. They offered me a plastic razor which might have been OK for ladies' armpits but would have just torn shreds out of my ten-day growth. I decided to stay hairy. Drunk and hairy. And very relieved.

I was met at Heathrow and taken straight to Whitehall to the Ministry of Defence to answer a series of embarrassing questions. I was still on the Army's reserve list which meant I wasn't supposed to go and live outside the country without informing the Army that I was leaving. Not cricket. They were a bit peeved, but the debriefing was matter-of-fact, which is the way it should be. Emotions should never enter into a debriefing, because you're trying to ascertain facts and sometimes facts go out of the window when emotions get involved. The man in charge of South American Affairs wanted to know what I was doing there. What was going on? Who did I see? Who did I talk to? How many Melvilles? What were their names? How old were they? Were there any Europeans there? Any Russians? What weapons did I see? Were there any Russian markings on them? He asked me who recruited me, and what publication I'd seen the ad in. At that point they were concerned that covert ads were going into the press to try to recruit mercenaries. But they were convinced in this case the ad wasn't part of a conspiracy to recruit mercenaries, despite the sinister Major Betancourt-Gomez, the Guyanese Catering Corps major I'd met at the Caledonian Hotel. They debriefed me there for a day. Then they let me go, and I phoned my mum.

She sent me some money and I flew back to Scotland. When I got home I phoned my fiancée Marion and said, 'You'd better come over here right away.' Poor Marion. She didn't know what she'd been missing. Then the next person I phoned was my friend Gavin Goodwin, who said, 'Lock yourself in your house. Don't talk to anybody. I want to come down and do a story.'

Gavin is a journalist who had written a story about me going to South America: 'Young Man Leaves Sweetheart to Seek Adventure . . .' Standard tabloid junk, only good for wrapping fish and chips in, but still I thought it only fair to offer him the chance of doing a follow-up. So he came and interviewed me and did another big story. When my mother read it in the paper the next day, she said, 'You never told me this.'

She thought I was still ten years old. She refused to believe I could be a South American revolutionary who went around killing people. And if I told her I didn't do it she'd believe me. It's a strange thing about women, and especially mothers. No matter what the evidence is, they always believe the best of their little boy. The number of times you've read about obvious villains who have perpetrated the most terrible crimes and their mothers say, 'He's a good boy. He would never have done such a thing.' I suddenly understood. Mothers believe what their sons tell them. It's a biological fact. She was just worried that the job hadn't worked out and I didn't have respectable references from my ex-bosses to go job-hunting again. One of the first things she said was, 'What are you going to do now?'

I said, 'I don't know. I think I'm going to marry Marion.' Which I did a couple of months later. My mother gave up trying to find jobs for me after that.

Belfast

Deep down inside I'm a very domesticated person, perfectly happy sitting in front of the television with a can of beer, a box of fried chicken and my feet up. Which is exactly what I was doing the night the IRA hit Cupar Street. One minute I was sitting there contentedly opening yet another beer, the next minute I'm watching BBC newsfilm of two of my blood-stained mates being carried out of an army ambulance into the emergency casualty ward of a hospital in Belfast.

Number 240 Cupar Street, Belfast, was a derelict house which had been fortified into an army patrol base in a quiet street just off the city centre and an IRA bomber had crept into the abandoned butcher's shop next door and piled a whole heap of explosives against the wall. I recognised the casualties on the TV news, Norrie Boyle and Stef Shemolensky. Blown up by terrorists. I'd been in Malaya with them, drunk with them, fought with them, fooled around with them. They were my friends. That's when I decided I was going back into the regiment.

It wasn't just Norrie and Stefan. I'd been missing the excitement of army life. Northern Ireland and the terrorist scene was a whole new can of worms. I'd been trained in conventional warfare, I'd fought in jungle warfare, but this was something I'd never been involved in, real urban guerilla warfare.

This wasn't the warfare of forced marches and massed

infantry battles or foot patrols slogging through swamps or jungles to attack or defend villages. This was war fought in terraced streets and bus stations and shopping centres, and a major battle would involve only a dozen men. Short of World War Three, or an undreamt of invasion of the Falklands, this was the future of war and I'd never forgive myself if I didn't experience it. It was total war on a small scale. And small is sometimes interesting.

And there were other things going on that made rejoining the Army seem attractive. Since getting back from Guyana in 1969, life had seemed a little bit flat. I'd married Marion, which was great, but marriage didn't exactly fit with my teenage ideas of playing the field and having a good time with the girls. I'd stayed on in Motherwell, where I managed a bar for a month or two. Then I moved south and ran a small hotel in London. In 1970 I was arrested in London for being in possession of pornography for gain. An old army buddy had been running a porno bookshop in Soho when he was caught with a bundle of US hundred-dollar bills which had been, how can I say it, printed locally. He was sent to jail for five years and he desperately needed someone to mind the store while he was away. It's not that I approve of dirty bookshops, but nobody else volunteered and I was fond of my comrade, so I took it on. It wasn't a clever move. I was busted on five occasions for having hard-core porn in the shop and I was due to go to Court. And I thought, well, I don't really fancy a future in the sex business, anyway. If I appeared in Court as a serving soldier, it would show I'd found an alternative career. I'd have some nice, upper-class officer from the regiment as a character witness and I could say the whole thing was a dreadful mistake. It should make the judge a lot more lenient.

And then there was the marriage. Marion was a former beauty queen, an ex-*Penthouse* Pet, and a stunning girl.

But I really got married for the wrong reasons. I got married because I thought it would be nice to have a kid. And we had a little girl, who's now a big girl. That was OK but the trouble was Marion wasn't really into marriage. Her own parents hadn't exactly hit it off and this prejudiced her. One night after the wedding we were driving through Edinburgh and I said, 'You're not worried about being married, are you, darling?' And she said, 'No, I've got all the money I need saved up for my divorce.' Dear me!

We stayed married for another futile five or six years, but it was really over when I volunteered to go to Northern Ireland. I told her I'd been ordered to go. And she was on the bus one day and this woman said to her, 'You must be very proud of John getting picked over all those other men who volunteered.' Well, as you can imagine, Marion wasn't exactly thrilled by this information. She thought I wanted to go to Ireland rather than stay with my wife and daughter. And she was right. That was what really broke my marriage. I had lied. I wanted to go to Northern Ireland. I knew she wouldn't understand, so I lied. Eight years later she finally got the divorce she had already saved up for before our honeymoon. Win some, lose some. I handled the whole thing very badly. I was quite immature at the time and it was a mess. So the Army was a way out.

Before I made it to Belfast, I had to undergo retraining and re-evaluation at the Guards' depot. And then I was sent to Germany to rejoin the regiment in Munster where they were part of the British Army of the Rhine.

The Regimental Sergeant Major looked through my previous army record, and the Ministry's confidential notes about my little escapade in Guyana and decided I had been a bad boy in the past and I might be a bad boy again. So he made me a corporal and put me in the regimental police force. It was a case of 'set a thief to catch a thief'. Also, they could keep an eye on me if I was in the police. It sounds like a position of trust but actually it meant that they still didn't quite trust me. However my attitude this time was a lot more mature. I wasn't just in the Army for kicks. I wanted to learn things. And if I was anti-authority it was because I thought authority was doing things the wrong way, not because I was being bloody-minded.

One day I was taking a soldier, a Grenadier Guard, for a shower. He was under arrest and had to have an escort between the shower room and his cell. When he stripped off, I saw track marks on his arm, so I reported this quietly to my sergeant. He didn't know what the hell I was talking about. The Army is so bound with tradition and so conservative that it clings to old virtues and vices long after they've been overtaken by the latest behaviour of the rest of society. The sergeant knew all about the military vices of alcohol, nicotine and various forms of fornication. But I had been in Civvy Street and I knew about drugs.

I suggested to the sergeant that we send the soldier discreetly to the medic for a routine examination. Just pretend it was for an FFI – Freedom from Infection certificate. It's quite usual, just a precaution against clap or headlice. The doctor phoned us straight back and confirmed what I thought. The doctor said the soldier had been injecting himself but he couldn't be sure what with. The sergeant was impressed. Suddenly I was an expert on drugs.

He reported it to the Adjutant and the SIB were called in, that's the Special Investigation Branch of the Military Police. Policing soldiers in the British Army is partly done by the regiments themselves and partly by the independent Regiment of Military Police. The two don't always work together as closely as they might. The SIB said they had a major drugs problem and they wanted me to help solve it. I was to infiltrate the junkie network.

Guardsmen and other squaddies used to go absent

without leave in Germany and they'd get hooked up with Germans and Americans. Dangerous activity because there were sensitive missile bases in Germany which the Americans manned jointly with us. There were a lot of drugs around, mostly emanating from the Americans on these bases. I began to get friendly with some of these Grenadiers. Only the Adjutant, the SIB and my own sergeant knew what I was doing. I was working in the battalion during the day, but at night they locked me up in the cells with the detainees and drug suspects. And the bad guys thought I was one of them.

At least I knew how to talk to them. You don't run a porno store in Soho and drink in the clubs there without getting the right terminology about 'joints' and 'jacking up' and 'smack' and 'blow'. One of the SIB investigators who was supposed to be fighting the drugs problem had asked me innocently, 'Well, what are they actually doing? Smoking marijuana cigarettes?' I almost passed out. He knew nothing.

'You know what smack is?' I asked him. 'Or horse?'

He looked puzzled. 'Two types of drugs?'

I said, 'No, it's just two ways of asking for the same thing, heroin.' I asked him some other questions and he confirmed my suspicions. He was just a soldier. He had no qualifications for being in the Drug Squad. So I was very useful.

One day I was walking down the street in Munster with one of the drug-using deserters. We were strolling around, going into bars, and we were both in civvies. He naturally thought I was AWOL too. Suddenly two military police guys leapt out and tried to arrest us both. They didn't know I was undercover.

We were just going into a bar called the Mini Sporting Club and the MPs jumped the guy I was with and one hell of a fight broke out. The squaddie was tackling both of them and I, well, I was in a difficult situation. The most important thing was not to have my cover blown, so I bolted. Behind me these MPs were shouting, 'Get him, stop him!' So the German police joined in and chased me through the main railway station, the Bahnhof. They even fired warning shots to persuade me to stop but I kept on running. Crazy! I'm dead against arming the police. I could have been killed.

Luckily they were lousy shots and I eventually made it back to the quarters of Tom Lindsay, my sergeant. I said, 'Tom, I'm a hunted man. They're chasing me everywhere. The *Polizei* have been shooting at me! Can you put me up for the night?' But Tom just drove me back to my own quarters and nothing happened. I was in the clear but it had been a close thing. I hadn't enjoyed it much. Tom, however, thought it was all the more reason for me to continue operating in secret.

Finally, through hanging around bars with these dropouts, keeping a wary eye out for MPs and *Polizei*, I was told where all the junkie absentees used to go. It was a German dope dealer's house, full of drugs. After two visits there myself, I went back to Tom Lindsay and told him what I'd found. That night the place was raided by the German civil police and the British military police and they grabbed ten absentees and about a quarter of a million dollars worth of dope. It was quite a coup and the authorities were very impressed.

Which was just as well, because a few days later, my pornography case came up. George Cooper, the sergeant major, called me into his office and asked, 'Do you know there's a warrant for your arrest in London?'

I said, 'No.'

He said, 'On charges of trafficking in pornography.'

I kept a straight face and said innocently, 'No' once again, and then I thought better of it and said, '. . . Oh, pornography, oh yes, that, ah, well actually I do remember something about that. It's all a terrible mistake.'

So George, who was actually on my side because he appreciated that my spell in the sleazy dives of Soho had actually paid some positive dividends for the Army, said, 'I'll tell you what I'll do. I'll keep you out here for another year with this battalion and when the Second Battalion comes, I'll have you transferred to them and you still won't have to go back. And maybe after that length of time they might drop the charges. Or, if you prefer, you can go back and face them.'

I said I'd go back and face them. I wanted to get it over with. It would have been torture having that hanging over me for years and years.

So I went back and they provided me with an officer to plead my case, just as I knew they would. I put on my medal ribbons and my best blues, I polished my toecaps and cap badge so that I looked a credit to my Queen and country. The officer told the Court, 'This man is back home with his regiment now, he's just been promoted, he's due for another promotion, he's doing very well. He's married with a child and this is an episode in his life he wants to put behind him.'

The judge just happened to be an ex-soldier. I wondered if, secretly, he was also into dirty books, because he fined me the minimum on each charge. Fifty pounds a time. And a few weeks later, back in Munster, I got the news I had been waiting for. We were being posted to Northern Ireland.

The rule was that everyone had to go, unless they were Irish. The British Army don't bother to boast about it, but there are thousands of patriotic citizens of the Irish Republic who serve quite happily and loyally as officers and squaddies in our regiments. They see it as in the best interests of both North and South in Ireland to defeat the terrorism of the Provisional IRA. But, because their families might be vulnerable to blackmail and retaliation, they aren't compelled to serve in Ulster.

Even so, there were enough deeply, deeply English and Scottish soldiers who had never set foot in the Emerald Isle, who suddenly discovered Irish 'roots' and used that as their excuse to stay on in Germany. Others, who were near the end of their tour, bought themselves out of the Army sooner than face four months in Ulster. They had enjoyed years of a comfortable foreign posting on the Rhine with only the risk of getting fat and flabby, and now they were being asked to do a soldier's job they were off with their tails between their legs.

But I was looking forward to it. Before we went, we had to go through a Northern Ireland training session which lasted for several weeks. The aim was to put us into stressful situations as near to the real thing as possible, sometimes too realistic. We had four men in our battalion killed in training, burned to death in an accident. And we rehearsed over and over and over again.

The difference between reacting well and reacting badly in a life or death emergency, is how often you practise. And in training they made sure there were real fights, real blood, real broken bones, because that was just a taste of what we were going to encounter in Belfast. At Senelage in Germany they had built a 'Tin City', a metal mock-up of houses, shops and pubs, which was laid out to look like the narrow streets and alleyways of Belfast. And they sent us out on endless patrols with mock briefings.

They'd give us a blurred Polaroid picture of a soldier who was playing the part of an IRA man and say, 'Make a sweep of McGinty's Bar. See if this man is there. If he is arrest him.' So a patrol of a dozen men, some with riot shields at the ready, would poke their heads round the door of the mock-up pub and they'd be faced with a hundred or so squaddies who had been told to act like mean drinkers who hated the sight of a British Army uniform. Now, here were soldiers being asked to behave like hooligans. It was like a godsend to them. They did this every payday anyway and got arrested for it, now they were being ordered to do it as part of their job.

They'd throw glasses and bottles as if they meant it. These guys really wanted to hurt you. When we located and snatched our 'IRA' suspect, we'd have to drag him by the hair or the legs across a room littered with broken glass and out into the street. They must have spent days in the hospital getting glass out of the bums of these guys. But as the glass had usually been thrown at us by their friends, I didn't have a great deal of sympathy.

They taught us riot control, how to seal off a city street and to use plastic bullets from $1\frac{1}{2}$-inch calibre launchers to beat back petrol-bomb throwers. They taught us how to act when the time came to use live, high velocity rounds against a mob of women and children being used as cover for snipers, how to hold fire until specific people were targeted and to try to drop them cleanly with a single shot.

They taught us how to search houses, starting with simple building surveying techniques to see if the building's measurements tallied both inside and outside. We found false walls, hidden closets and bookcases with secret storage spaces. We found the legs of chairs neatly drilled and plugged after a couple of rounds of ammo had been hidden inside.

We also learned how to frisk people thoroughly. Most people seem to think a search on a person is to lift their arms, pat under their arms down to their waist, down each leg and that's it. They've missed the obvious places; the small of the back, the back of the neck and the crotch. You can't afford to be shy about searching a guy's balls. For some reason men think it's not macho to put a hand down and grope around the crotch. When I was instructing, I would always have some sort of contraband down the front of my underpants. My pupils never found it. They never looked for it. They thought groping round my testicles was faggoty behaviour and they weren't going to

71

take the risk. By not doing so, they took a much bigger risk.

You are also taught to search people's hair and behind their ears. A detonator, for instance, is only about three inches long and as thick as a pencil. And it's as important to find a detonator as it is to find a ton of explosives. Without a detonator, that ton of explosives is useless.

And we learned how to gather the raw material to feed the Army's intelligence computers which piece together the jigsaw of Irish terrorism. The information for the computers mainly came from P-checks, stop and search personal interrogation or house searches. The aim was to build up a complete computer dossier on every terrorist suspect.

During a routine house search, each soldier would be given a specific task of memorising details of a specific room in the house. After the search every little detail was fed into the computer and every little detail, however trivial, was important. We'd describe the colour of the front door, the furniture inside each room, the carpets, the family photos above the fireplace. Now, say three weeks later, a routine patrol in Londonderry, who know their own patch inside out, find a stranger wandering in their area. They take him aside and question him and he claims he lives at a Belfast address. The patrol ask for a quick P-check on the radio and then challenge the stranger to describe his own front door at home, or his bedroom rug. It was amazing how many people couldn't describe their own house – and ended up in secure interrogation cells because of that.

We were shown, without pulling any punches, the evidence of the tactics of the terrorists we were going to face. Film of Belfast girls tarred and feathered by IRA thugs for being friendly with soldiers, and photographs of victims who had been 'kneecapped' for revealing the truth about terrorism. Their tendons were ripped and poking

72

out through a bloody mass of bone, smashed by the force of a bullet or chewed into pulp by the tip of a tungsten masonry bit in a Black and Decker drill. They faced life in a wheelchair. Or the charred and twisted remains of the innocent bomb victims, barely recognisable as human beings, indiscriminately killed as if in an orgy of sadism.

I was reminded grotesquely of an incident when I was a child in Africa. I used to breed white mice. I had over a hundred of them in a big box about four feet long with three tiers. It was a sort of cottage industry and I'd sell them at school. A cat killed them all. I came out of the house one morning and the whole lawn was covered with dead mice – day-olds, week-olds, all my mice gone. I think that put me off cats for life. It's one thing to kill in self defence, or for food, but to kill for pleasure like a cat does . . . I've never thought that was terribly nice. Unattractive in humans too. Don't get me wrong, I'm not making a joke of it. There *are* people who kill for pleasure.

In Germany, at the training camp, it was all theory. In Northern Ireland the theory was put to the test, but they couldn't prepare us for the menace and the boredom and the real risks of the streets in Belfast, and the sheer hatred most of the Catholics felt for us. Who could have prepared me for the homely old granny waiting at the pedestrian crossing on the corner of Falls Road, the first day I was on patrol? I offered to help her across, and she turned and saw my cap badge and insignia. She looked up at me and grabbed my arm and said, 'Oh, you're a Guardsman. We prefer Guardsmen on duty up the Falls.' I thought she was grateful for our professionalism and our impartiality and our ability to keep the peace. Like hell she was. She stared into my eyes and said, 'Guardsmen are a lot taller than other Brit soldiers and they make easier targets for our boys.' She spat on the pavement and hobbled away. I knew then that this was Belfast and you couldn't trust anyone, not a stooped old granny or a schoolkid or a parish priest.

I settled into the routine of patrolling and quickly learned that the veterans who had done Belfast before had come up with their own answers to the Irish Question. In return for the hatred of the locals, you gave them harassment. The Army commanders in the comfortable officers' messes back at headquarters and the politicians in the bars and clubs at Westminster were always going on about winning the hearts and minds of the Catholic community in Belfast. My attitude to hearts and minds was a little more cynical. Blow their minds and break their hearts was my motto.

Inevitably there were a lot of complaints about how we treated these people. I got into trouble once over a suicide attempt. A guy came running up to us on patrol and shouted, 'Jesus! Come quick, there's a poor man about to commit suicide. You've got to save him.' We followed him round the corner, wary that we were walking into an ambush from a sniper in Divis Flats across the street. But, sure enough, there was an idiot at the window of a terraced house, two floors up, just twenty feet off the ground, threatening to jump. Now, how much damage can you do from that height? So I deployed my patrol and shouted up to him, 'What are you doin' up there?'

He said, 'I'm gonna jump.'

And I said, 'Well, if you're gonna jump, then jump, 'cos I'm a busy man and I don't have all day to spend waiting around while you make up your mind.'

He jumped. And he broke his legs and a few other odds and ends as well. But he lived, as I'd known he would. I told his neighbours to get him into a car and take him to hospital. My men were being forced to stand around in the middle of a hostile crowd in a hostile area where they were at risk. I wanted them back on patrol, pronto.

But, oh, the complaints that came in. The neighbours complained, the shopkeepers complained, the parish priest complained and the stooped old granny even got her own word in. And I ended up in front of the CO. So I told him that my attitude was that nothing I could say was going to make the man jump, or stop him jumping, and I just wanted it over before somebody shot one of my men. So the guy jumped and broke a couple of legs. Big deal. None of my men got shot. As far as I was concerned, I came out ahead. I was a sergeant in the British Army, not a Samaritan.

If there was mutual malice between us and the locals, there was a blood vendetta between us and the Provisionals. We looked on it as a battle to the death, but, because of the politicians and army rules and regulations, we were fighting with one hand tied behind our backs. Of course we're human, and when we thought nobody was looking, we untied that other hand and played it just as dirty as the Provisionals. A lot of the guys carried 'Belfast Spares'. You go out on patrol with your self-loading rifle and a full magazine of twenty rounds of ammo. But you carry a single spare round, usually in the breast pocket. The old joke was that in a Catholic/Protestant holy war in Ireland, you carried a bullet in your pocket, over your heart, so if anybody fired a Bible at you the bullet would break the impact and save your life.

It might be late at night, on a dark street, when you spot some Provisional hard-line terrorist with a gun, or even some teenage errand-runner carrying a weapon between Provo 'safe houses'. Now the rules say that you've got to shout out a challenge to the gunman and give him a warning that you're a soldier. That's just bullshit. The very least that's going to happen is the guy's gonna get away, if he doesn't panic.

And then a few night's later he's gonna see you before you see him and you or one of your mates is dead. Or when you challenge him he's gonna turn and shoot first. But if you've got the insurance of a spare round, and you're *sure* the guy's carrying a piece, *you* get to shoot first. And then you start a few seconds of screaming and challenging. And you fire a second round in the air. By the time reinforcements have arrived and the area is sealed off, you've got your spare out of your pocket and loaded it in your rifle magazine. So back at headquarters, when the de-brief and inquest session starts, they take your gun and count the ammo and they accept that you've only fired one round.

Everybody for miles around has heard a shot, then shouting, then another shot. And you'd tell them that you'd been on patrol and somebody had fired on you, and maybe there might have been a couple of them, and you had yelled a warning and returned fire and hit one of them. And if they had a dead Provo on their hands, and his weapon, it didn't matter if his gun had been fired or not. And you could be back on patrol the next night and you'd made the streets a little safer.

I saw a double bonus one night when there was a drunken brawl. Two guys were having a fight up an alleyway. We heard the report on the radio and went over. One of the squaddies on patrol got the two guys up against a wall, searched them and found weapons. To the amazement of everybody he said, 'Go on, get lost, don't let me catch you doing this again.' And he gave them the weapons back. As they ran off up the alleyway, he shot them both dead. In the report it was said we could see they were in possession of weapons and they had ignored our warnings. We were all congratulated for our quick reactions.

Another time three of us were doing a Vehicle Check Point when a car came down the street, three guys in it, and refused to stop. A shot was fired at us and they sped away. Two of my men opened fire on the car. They killed one person and badly wounded another. The car crashed about fifty or sixty yards away, and before we could get to it, there were 100 people around that car. We couldn't force a way through without starting a serious riot, so the locals took the three guys out of the car and got them off to hospital. They also took any weapons out of the car. The next day there's a major complaint filed against the British Army for shooting unarmed youths. It's a dirty little war in Belfast.

But occasionally, only very rarely, we got straight results and some satisfaction when the Provos self-destructed. We were patrolling the Clonard area in our PIG, that's a five-ton Humber armoured vehicle called a PIG because it looks like one – long, square and with a big snout. We were squinting through the slits in the side, the gun ports, watching out for any unusual activity, when I spotted a guy I thought I recognised from the Muppet Show. This was the line-up of mugshots back in the briefing room at company headquarters, a wall covered with head and shoulders photos of wanted IRA suspects. Some of the photos were copies of passport pictures, sent straight to the Army by passport office clerks in Belfast and London. Others were slightly out of focus telephoto shots taken at demos or funerals or riots. And some were from the files of the Royal Ulster Constabulary interrogation centre at Castelreagh. You could always tell those. Perfect focus and lighting, full face and profile, but you had to use your imagination a little because the suspect was usually shown with a black eye or a swollen lip.

Anyway, this guy in Clonard looked familiar, and suspicious, so we pulled the PIG over and shouted for him to stop. He ran off around the corner so we chased him on foot and cornered him in an alleyway. He wasn't a very impressive character. A sleazy little weasel of a man. I didn't think he was big enough to be a gunman. He was more like a thief, one of these little men who would carry guns and ammo for others.

We took him off for questioning. I was sitting beside the driver, and this little guy was in the back, with a soldier on either side of him. He was dead nervous and fidgety. Obviously he'd heard stories about what the Brits did to people like him. We were driving along when there was this incredible WHOOF in the back of the PIG and the little guy lifted about two feet from his seat and seemed to burst out of his jacket and then collapsed on the floor. It looked like the worst case of haemorrhoids I'd ever seen. Blood everywhere. We drove him straight to the Victoria Hospital where the medics signed him dead on arrival.

They diagnosed that he'd hidden a fulminate of mercury detonator up his arse. Detonators are funny things. Sometimes they won't ignite no matter how much electricity you put through them and sometimes they'll explode just from the heat of your hand. So once he'd hidden it where he did, he'd more or less signed his own death warrant. It wasn't a pretty way to go. He'd died of internal bleeding within seconds. That's the reality of the situation out there, a lot of distinctly unglamorous deaths.

I came close to an unglamorous death myself in the Great Falls Road Chip Shop Disaster. It was the night the piss hit the pan. The IRA had set up Incident Centres in houses and little offices all over the Lower Falls, where local people could go and file complaints against the Army, claiming everything from furniture being smashed during house searches to underwear being stolen off the washing line. We reckoned that at least some of these Incident Centres were being used to store weapons or as safe houses for gunmen on the run, but we needed cast-iron evidence before raiding any of them. So we set up a covert observation post to watch one of the Incident Centres, just opposite a popular fish and chip shop in the Lower Falls. The chip shop was ideally situated, one of a row of shops and offices at street level in a terrace, with abandoned and derelict flats above.

Under the cover of darkness, it took a few hours and

three different patrols to get us in position. Each of the patrols had an extra man on duty as they set off. Five men would enter the alleyway behind the chip shop and only four would come out the other end. The fifth man would scuttle up the rear steps and into the derelict flat we had chosen. We did it in the early hours of the morning, when the chip shop and the offices were closed. I was first in, after I'd quietly forced off the wooden board which had been nailed over the door. Within a couple of hours two other Guardsmen had joined me. We wedged the door closed behind us and settled down for the next three days, with pre-cooked cold rations and ziploc plastic bags to use as portable field latrines.

By daylight next morning we were ready, blackened up with camouflage face cream, hiding in the shadows a few feet back from the window, taking photos of everyone who went in and out of the Incident Centre in the house opposite. A couple of nights later disaster struck. It was Friday night, the busiest night in the chip shop. One of the plastic latrine bags had burst, unknown to us, and the contents were dripping down through the ceiling into the shop. It was hitting the hot fat in the deep pan fryer and going 'psssh'.

There was a queue of hungry people out as far as the door and they began to shrink back against the wall as these drips began to splatter searing fat over the counter. Now nobody smelled anything unusual about this stream of liquid, but there you are. And the wife of the owner looked up and said, 'Holy Mother of God, there's a leaking pipe up there Seamus, you'd better go and sort it out.'

When we heard Seamus coming up the stairs the three of us got behind the door. Seamus gave one heave with his shoulder to free the wooden wedge, and we jerked the door open, grabbed him into the empty flat, put the muzzle of a Browning 9mm automatic in his mouth, and handcuffed him. Our observation post was blown. I grabbed the radio and whispered our 'Breakout' code into it. An armoured PIG was constantly on patrol in the neighbourhood and the crew had a list of locations for our hiding places. They knew from our panic 'Breakout' message that we needed to be rescued – fast. The PIG came roaring round the corner from North Howard Street, promptly rammed into a car and traffic ground to a halt for blocks around. In the meantime the drips of piss had turned into a steady trickle and with hot fat spraying out of the deep pan in the direction of the gas burners, the customers began to get seriously terrified and Seamus's wife lost her patience.

She asked them, 'Will you be hanging on just a while and I'll see what's keeping that stupid bugger Seamus?' So she plodded up the stairs and found herself bundled into the empty flat and staring down a gun barrel as we handcuffed her as well. By this time I'm yelling the breakout code into the radio and listening to the explosive spluttering of cold piss and hot fat, and smelling the smoky fumes drifting up through the floor. From the window we could see the customers retreating back into the street, waiting for the explosion and fireball.

Finally the PIG screamed into the alleyway and we piled in, taking Seamus and his wife with us. We couldn't afford to leave them behind to raise the alarm. But a couple of minutes later we dumped them in the street outside our base, took off the cuffs and let them walk back to their shop.

In the meantime some local hero had realised that if the chip shop burst into flames it would probably take out most of the houses around, together with the parish church and the primary school. A chip shop fire has got about the same destructive yield as a small nuclear device. If you don't believe me, ask any insurance investigator. So the hero crept in, at great personal risk, and switched off the gas burners. Then he got trampled in the rush of hungry looters. By the time Seamus and his wife got back, the piss was sizzling gently and the fat was cooling. But all the stock was gone – cod, plaice, chips, pickles, soft drinks, cigarettes. Even the one-armed bandit in the corner had vanished, probably on its way to a patriotic Republican drinking club.

Seamus and his wife were first in the queue at the Incident Centre across the street next morning and they whacked in a compensation bill to the Army. I sometimes wonder if the Army paid it in full. It would have been cheap at the price. I had stayed with the smoking chip shop to the last possible minute, like a captain reluctant to leave his sinking ship, but the whole incident was a shameful blot on my career. Still, the last thing I wanted was an epitaph which said: 'John Miller, soldier, Guyanese rebel and terrorist fighter – died in a chip pan fire, Belfast 1974.'

In my first tour of Ulster we had a company of a hundred men. In four months we had four men killed and the remaining ninety-six of us sustained a total of 142 reported gunshot wounds. You don't have to be Einstein to figure out that some people were getting shot more than once. But I couldn't have done too badly. When that tour of Belfast was over, we went back to Germany and the following year I was asked to go back to Ulster, in plain clothes, undercover, attached to Military Intelligence.

I was sent to a country house in Nottinghamshire where they put me through a lot of different types of tests. I was locked in a compound and asked to escape. I had to cross raging torrents, evade tracker dogs, live off berries and wild animals. All that sort of thing. They were keen on depriving me of sleep and then suddenly confronting me with a whole range of command decisions. It was supposed to determine whether your logical reasoning powers could withstand pressure, to find out what your psychological stress threshold was. My part, this time round, was to be in basic intelligence gathering – plain clothes undercover at the front line, not deep cover in the background.

The Army had scored some great successes and suffered some disasters in the intelligence field. A couple of years before I arrived, Army Intelligence had literally been taking in the IRA's dirty washing, with spectacular results. One of the Belfast units of the Military Reaction Force, had dreamt up the Army's most secret and successful intelligence operations. The members of the unit, which included a couple of army girls, had been through background rehearsals and elocution lessons until they could pass themselves off as Belfast locals.

They were given their own secure flat in Belfast and a small business office near the city centre, where they ran the Four Square Laundry. The laundry business was a smash hit from the beginning. One undercover soldier drove the laundry van while another spied from a concealed compartment above the driver's cab. The girls went from door to door in the most hard-line terrorist housing estates of West Belfast, handing out leaflets, introducing their new service. There was a special cut-price deal on dry cleaning gents' suits, shirts, trousers and casual jackets. Rock-bottom prices, for a limited period only, hurry, hurry, get your bargains now! And the housewives of Belfast handed in their men's clothes at the beginning of the week and got them back, immaculately laundered and pressed, forty-eight hours later.

It was service with more than a smile, the secret owners of the Four Square Laundry could hardly keep from laughing out loud. Each laundry bag was neatly tagged with the owner's name and address. Back in the Central Belfast office the bags were re-labelled with fake names, switched to an unmarked van and driven to a clandestine forensic unit at Aldergrove Airport. Every item of clothing was 'paraffin-tested', a swift and simple chemical test which can show up traces of gunpowder and explosive residue on the clothes of anyone who has fired a weapon. The clothes were then loaded into an RAF Hercules and flown to an English base. Then they were delivered to a commercial dry-cleaning company, who were told they were being given a trial contract for servicemen's family laundry. The clothes were beautifully cleaned, on over-time rates, and air-freighted back to Belfast.

A week or so later, the proud owners of newly cleaned jackets, which had shown traces of powder, were being arrested at bus stops and social security offices and pubs. And they never twigged. Terrorists were being targeted at an enormous rate and, given the lack of business overheads on their official accounts, the Four Square Laundry was turning in a healthy profit.

But it all came to a grisly end. It was inevitable that the Provisionals should start to take an interest in the flourishing Four Square operation. Not because they suspected it was an intelligence front but because it was a promising looking business and it wasn't paying protec-tion money to the IRA. Republican patriotism in Ulster is one-tenth politics and nine-tenths straight money-making gangsterism for the big boys in the Movement. Every pub, club, taxi, video shop and building site has to pay them protection money.

The Four Square Laundry would happily have handed over its entire income in protection money. But round about the same time, an informer, a tout, who knew about the operation, slipped away from his Army minders and blew the secret to the Provos. It was whispered in Intelli-gence circles that the tout had once been taken for a ride in the hidden compartment above the driver's cab of the laundry van, to spot 'faces' in the neighbourhood for his minders, and he knew the whole routine. When the van went out on its next run, it was ambushed. One IRA man shot the driver and another let a burst from an automatic into the bodywork above the cab. He watched happily as blood oozed from the bullet holes in the metal. It was a warning to us all about the dangers of ever trusting a tout.

However, it wasn't all bad news, and the Army got a good result out of the Great Portadown Train Crash. In November 1974 the IRA stopped the Dublin–Belfast mail train south of the Ulster border and forced the driver and guard off at gunpoint. Then they set the train going again, driverless and with the throttle wide open, heading for Belfast. The plan was that the train would plough into the main station in Belfast at full speed at the height of the morning rush hour and scare everybody shitless.

The Army got plenty of warning and they got out the map of the rail route. The panic was over almost as soon as it had begun. About thirty miles south of Belfast is the town of Portadown where the rail line curves sharply and it was obvious the locomotive, travelling at 100 m.p.h. would never make the bend. Better still, the Army calculated, it should come off the line around Obins Street, a notorious Republican area. A great propaganda victory for the Army if the train never made it as far as Belfast but instead threatened the lives of innocent Catholic women and children in Portadown.

The train duly came off the lines, helped a little by an army specialist who loosened the track and sleepers at a strategic spot. It smashed into the bridge at Obins Street, and the army trucks toured round the area warning that mindless IRA terrorists could have killed everybody in the neighbourhood and that they'd better get out of their houses because the Army had been warned there was a 1,000-lb bomb on board the train.

Hundreds of Catholic families legged it to safety and road blocks were put up once the area was cleared. Then, while the houses were empty, the Army had a field day. They trucked in squads of snoopers who had been trained at our special unit of the Intelligence Centre in Ashford, Kent, which taught lock-picking and burglary. Dozens of houses were taken apart and searched and carefully put back together again. The searchers couldn't have resisted the temptation to leave behind the odd round of ammo hidden expertly under a sink or on top of a cupboard, for a rainy-day arrest, as it were.

Then there was the Antrim Road brothel run by the Army, where the girls and the business expertise were provided by a well-known Maltese villain who controlled most of the vice rackets in the West End of London. The British Army took over the running of the brothel and we bugged the bedrooms. These guys were getting hand jobs and blow jobs, and giving away bedroom secrets at the same time. It was useful for blackmail too. And we took photographs.

There was wickedly effective black propaganda. When a two-man Provisional team pulled a bank raid in Belfast, they got away with £8,000. We put the word out that the haul had actually been £12,000. That weekend both bank robbers were found lying on a rubbish tip, shot through the back of the head. The Belfast Commander of the Provisionals put out the word that any other raiders who held back loot to line their own pockets would be dealt with in the same way.

Also the SAS. Just mention those initials and the Provos shit themselves. The SAS are absolutely ruthless, because they have to be. Their tactics are calculated to make the blood run cold. I think the action in Gibraltar showed that.

An SAS man moving in for the kill, will always finish off his target with a couple of bullets in the head. Sure, it's one way to make certain your target isn't going to get back up if you've spread his brains out on the pavement. A rifle bullet ripping a hole in the torso from two hundred metres away might do that job just as well, but a bullet in the face causes a lot of extra grief. It robs the Provos of the propaganda funeral with the brave, dead Volunteer lying in state for the cameras in an open coffin. The coffin lid has to be kept firmly shut if the dear departed has died at the hands of the SAS. But I didn't have to get involved in that sort of skulduggery. My job was mainly dealing with touts.

After I had passed the course in Nottinghamshire, we were all given three or four weeks' leave before going undercover. And the amazing thing was, almost everybody used this period to grow a droopy Zapata moustache – remember when those moustaches were in? And sideburns. But you can't grow your hair to any proper length in three or four weeks, so what you had was a stream of so-called undercover agents looking like pubescent Mexicans. All the Irishmen knew they were soldiers undercover. It was a dead giveaway.

There was no way in the world I was going to walk about like that and so I had my left ear pierced. I must have been the first person in the British Army to walk into barracks wearing an ear-ring. And I had a seriously short haircut. I was practically scalped. It created quite a stir but nobody ever whispered behind my back, 'He's an undercover soldier' because I couldn't possibly have looked any less like somebody from the Brigade of Guards. I worked from Army HQ in Lisburn and on trips into Belfast I passed myself off as an ex-rugby player promoting rock 'n' roll bands.

My partner Spike and I had a few successes. We ran some well-connected touts and we helped set up a few decent arms busts. The informers were passed on to us as a result of tip-offs from confidential telephone hotlines to the Army and police, or as a follow-up to a brisk interrogation at Castlereagh of a suspect whose nerve had cracked. We did so well in the first few operations that we held back a small surplus of pistols in our secure store at Lisburn so we could ration those out during the lean times to make it look as if we were being consistently successful.

As for the touts, we never completely trusted them. Bearing in mind the fate of the Four Square Laundry, we were being justifiably cautious. Many of our touts were IRA men who had been turned and we paid them in hard cash – hundreds of pounds a time – whenever they came up with good information for us. And we had some Protestant touts who wanted to grass up Protestant terrorist groups. That called for a few white lies on our part. The para-military cops, the Royal Ulster Constabulary, the only fully armed civilian police force in Britain, were always willing to be briefed in advance and provide back-up when we raided Catholic houses.

If you briefed them in advance on a Protestant raid, you'd be empty-handed when you bust down the door. There were just too many sympathetic RUC men who would make a warning phone call to your target. We needed their help in arrests, so we just adopted the tactic of giving them a false address for the raid. And once we had them in support in the general area, we'd switch to the real target at the last minute and they'd just have to go along with us and arrest their old mates.

No one ever identified Spike or me as undercover soldiers and only a couple of very senior army men knew our real identities and mission. One night Spike and I went into a bar to meet a tout who was supposed to give us some information. After a while a guy came up to Spike, not the guy we'd come to meet, and pulled him into the bathroom. As he reached inside his jacket, Spike pulled his gun out, whacked the guy over the head, kicked the door open and shouted for me. I bounded over, grabbed this guy, ran him right out to our car, helped Spike throw him in the back seat and drove off. God knows what the other customers thought was going on. But nobody's ever surprised by anything in a Belfast pub.

Spike stuck his gun in the guy's mouth. The man was trying to say he was Special Branch but Spike wouldn't believe him. Then we ripped open his jacket and found his gun and his ID. Royal Ulster Constabulary. He was pulling Spike in because he had seen him earlier in the bar talking to a known IRA man and he thought Spike was IRA. He'd obviously been reaching into his jacket for his ID when he'd pulled Spike into the bathroom. It was very embarrassing, but, though we'd seen his ID, he hadn't seen anything from us. He didn't know who we were, so we just slowed down, Spike opened the door and said, 'Goodnight' and threw him in the street.

Unfortunately somebody saw his sudden departure from the car and an alert went out saying, 'A green Cortina, two males, etc., etc.' And we got stopped in a vehicle check point. 'Out of the car, gentlemen.' So we got out of the car and they searched us and found our weapons. Suddenly everyone in the patrol was pointing a rifle at us. They took us back to an RUC station, where we completely refused to speak to anyone until we were interviewed by a very senior officer of brigade rank. We never carried any ID on undercover work but it was easy for the officer to check our serial numbers on the army computer and we were back on the streets again.

The work was varied and demanding, but I could sense that Spike's mind wasn't totally on the job and that worried me. I needed his undivided attention if we were to stay alive and successful. Then he explained his problem. When we were posted to Belfast, he had left his wife behind in married quarters in Germany and she had fallen into a torrid affair with the manager of the base NAAFI, which stands for Navy, Army and Air Force Institute who run the services' clubs and shopping centres. Spike knew what was going on and he was brooding about it. So, to preserve his peace of mind and my safety, I agreed he should make a secret trip back to Germany to sort out the problem. We dipped into our touts' fund, saying we needed two hundred quid to pay a tout for telling us where a gun was hidden.

Spike took the money, drove our undercover car with fake licence plates to Dublin, jumped on a plane and went to Germany. But this wasn't a man-to-man confrontation. In the early hours of the morning when the NAAFI manager locked up and was walking across the darkened parade ground to the married quarters, Spike jumped out of the bushes and beat the shit out of him. Then he got back to the airport, flew to Dublin, jumped in the car and was back in Lisburn before the NAAFI manager had coughed out enough broken teeth to tell the military police that his mystery assailant had been Spike.

They checked company records and found that Spike was on special assignment. They didn't bother to check him out any further since they knew he wasn't in Germany. They told the NAAFI manager that his guilty conscience had caused a case of mistaken identity and warned him to stop drinking so much and give up screwing Spike's wife.

About six weeks later, when the manager had fully recovered from his injuries, Spike got to brooding again and we raided the touts' fund for another couple of hundred quid and he made another lightning raid on Germany and beat the NAAFI manager to a pulp. Spike was a much happier man and more relaxed in his work when he got back. This time we got a gentle inquiry from the Intelligence controllers asking if we were going about our business and checking in regularly. And we told them we were on the trail of a safe house where some machine-guns were stored. They didn't bother us again after that. When the swelling and blood blisters went down under the NAAFI manager's eyes, the military police told him he needed a complete rest and an eye test and they said they might even investigate him because it looked like some vengeance attack from a German black marketeer and the manager had better watch his step.

But the third time Spike went to ambush his wife's lover, we nearly came unstuck. We had raided our entire illicit stockpile of spare ammo and captured Star pistols to trade them in for cash to cover Spike's expenses for his crimes of passion. He'd made good the first leg of his escape back from Germany and through Dublin but he was still a couple of hours short of base when Intelligence Corps phoned up from Germany and asked to speak to him. I did one of my funny accents and said, 'Not here.' Then they asked to speak to Sergeant Miller and I said I wasn't there either and that I must be out with Spike.

As soon as Spike drove the car back through the gates, I phoned Germany back and said we had just returned to barracks and what did they want. They wanted to know where Spike and I had been and I blew my top. Hush-hush, highly sensitive, infiltration of an I R A cell and all that, and we certainly weren't going to divulge any details because our tout would end up on a rubbish tip with a hood over his head and a bullet in his brain. There was an embarrassed silence and they apologised for doubting me and explained in total confidence that the N A A F I manager was in hospital yet again suffering this time with broken fingers and severely swollen testicles. They said, with an air of frustrated bewilderment, that this beaten and broken man had insisted on several occasions that Spike had materialised out of thin air and attacked him.

I thought about it and told them that this was obviously an extreme guilt syndrome which manifested itself in self-mutilation and they'd better mount a round-the-clock guard on the N A A F I manager because he would prob-ably commit suicide and leave a note blaming Spike for murder. But I don't think they believed me entirely, so I had to tell Spike to stop beating this man up, otherwise he was going to get caught and it would end up in a court-martial for both of us. Besides, the tour of Belfast was coming to an end and we were rejoining our own outfit and setting off for exercises in Canada. Even Spike couldn't have flown the Atlantic, committed grievous bodily harm on the NAAFI manager and made it back up the Rockies without somebody commenting on his absence.

It was in Medicine Hat in Canada that I ended my partnership with Spike and decided to end my partnership with the Army. We had been practising anti-tank drill, how to knock out a tank with a new American 66mm rocket launcher. The launchers come pre-loaded with one round in them, you fire that one shot and throw them away. In the lessons we had been using un-loaded demonstration models. Spike took his section of soldiers off for a rocket launching lesson and I was watching out of the corner of my eye as he pressed the back of his launcher against his thigh. Then he must have pressed the tit. There was an almighty flash and an incredible bang. Spike had been demonstrating with a live, loaded rocket launcher.

I was the first person to reach him. There was a hole where his leg had been. The smell was nauseating but luckily for Spike the back-blast had almost cauterised the wound and he wasn't bleeding as badly as he might have been. Luckily we were able to get a medical evacuation helicopter very fast and Spike survived. I was the biggest person with the same blood group, so I sat next to him in the chopper back to Medicine Hat, giving him a blood transfusion. He and I were the closest of friends anyway but we were even closer after that.

A few months later we were both back in England at Headley Court Rehabilitation Centre. I was having metal plates put in my arm after an accident of my own and Spike was being fitted with an artificial leg. I looked around at the other army casualties, men wounded and disfigured and I knew the Army would hold no future for most of them even after their injuries were patched up and healed. I knew too that it held no future for me. It was 1976. I had had enough of the Army. I had done Northern Ireland. I was a sergeant. I had achieved all my serious ambitions. The Army is a young man's life and I was over thirty. It was time to move on again.

Rock 'n' Punk

I became a rock 'n' punk tycoon by accident. Like all the best success stories, I was struggling to earn a living one minute, and absolutely rolling in cash the next.

There's one casual job that's usually always available to prevent fit young ex-soldiers filling too many places on the dole queue. Pubs and clubs need bouncers as the first line of defence on the door, and to mingle inside with the customers, with a quick eye to spot trouble developing, and enough muscle to put down an outbreak of fighting before it degenerates into general mayhem. The turnover in bouncers is pretty high because it's not much of a career for anyone, so there's no great problem getting a job like that to keep body and soul together until something better comes along.

That's what I was doing when I went along to see the management of Crackers club in Wardour Street a few months after I'd left the Army for the second time. Crackers was a run-of-the-mill disco club which was hardly ever filled to its 650-body capacity. It only opened five nights a week, from Tuesday to Saturday, but it could get lively enough to need a small team of minders to keep the mob at bay whenever they had a headline act who attracted troublesome fans.

The Friday night when I pitched up there, the club was less than half full and the two guys on the door, backed up by two others lounging near the bar, were more than enough to cope with any hassle from the bored customers who were lounging against the walls listening to some less than memorable group of equally bored rockers on stage.

I was giving the management a sales pitch, bullshitting about how I had a squad of trained anti-riot experts at my command and how we could provide a quick reaction force to ensure that good order would be maintained if the customers ever got too enthusiastic and surged out of hand. I was having about as much success as trying to offer a platoon of muscle-bound minders for a James Galway recital and I was definitely getting the 'Don't call us, we'll call you' signals from the manager, until my fellow Scots came to the rescue.

One of the doormen, a hulking great guy well able to look after himself, came hurrying up to the bar to see the boss. He looked nervous and worried as hell. The boss was suddenly overcome with the same frightened expression after the doorman whispered a few words in his ear.

'Shit. I wish you had your team of heavies with you now, John,' he said. 'I couldn't afford the expense of using your boys at the best of times, or the worst of times, but I could really do with them now.'

The sources of his potential problems were already reeling around the cashier's desk, breathing obscenities and alcohol fumes at the remaining besieged doorman. There were three of them, tartan scarves, blood-red eyes, the advance guard of a mob of about thirty other Jocks crazed with blood-lust and the taste for strong drink. They were that most dangerous breed of beast – Scottish foot-ball fans in London for a Wembley international game against the old enemy, the English.

By this time the customers inside could hear the growl-ing of drunken Scottish accents and were beginning to drink up and drift towards the emergency exits. The bar staff were clearing away as many empty glasses as possible and getting the takings out of the till and into the safe in the back office. An average night's marginally profitable custom at Crackers was about to turn into a considerable operating loss. And then there would be the insurance claims for furniture and fittings, and temporary replacements for the staff who would end up in the casualty wards.

I thought there might be a chance for me to impress the boss with my masterful command of a crisis situation, so I wandered over to the front door and prepared myself for action. I thought, with the back-up of the two doormen, we might be able to subdue the three drunks already trying to force their way into the club even if it meant slinging their arses into the gutter.

But it was already too late. The rest of the mob had rounded the corner of Wardour Street and were already in sight of the club. If their three mates came flying out of the doorway with bloody noses and loose teeth, they'd be bound to notice, and there was no way we'd be able to cope with the onslaught that would follow. So, not for the first time, I decided to see if I could talk my way out of trouble.

I turned my attention to the ringleader, an ugly brute almost the same height as me, with a livid scar down his left cheek, probably the result of some skirmish on the terraces of a football ground. 'Listen,' I said in a most reasonable manner, matching the thickness of my Scots accent to his, 'we're not looking for any trouble here. There's still time for a few more drinks in the Soho pubs. This is just a quiet wee club that charges fancy prices for its drinks.'

He was on tiptoe, looking over my shoulder into the darkness of the club, his eyes trying to focus on a couple of giggling little tarts whose wimp boyfriends would have been no match for the winning ways of a drunken Scot with a week's oil rig wages burning a hole in his pocket and a taste for soft English flesh. 'I'm no' worried aboot the prices,' he was saying. 'And if me and my mates want to come in and see for oorselves, who's gonnae stop us?'

The approach of the mob was now imminent. I had got myself into a sort of synchronised side step, moving a foot or so each way with the lurching rhythm of the drunk to prevent him bolting past me into the club. But he was right. Short of starting a bloodbath in the street, there was no way we could stop this mob sweeping us aside. And anyway barring him from coming inside was a dangerous insult to his Caledonian pride. So I tried a different approach. 'No,' I said. 'You're quite right, we couldn't stop you. It's actually your mates I'm worried about, they don't look as if they can hold their drink. And if they caused any trouble we'd have to call the cops and all hell would be let loose. It's Friday night and if anybody gets arrested they couldn't get to Court until Monday. They'd have to stay banged up in the cells for the weekend and they'd miss the chance to see Scotland beating England at Wembley tomorrow. Now, you and your two pals look like sensible people to me so I'll do a deal. Get rid of that bunch of loonies coming down the street and the three of you can come back here for free drinks.'

He thought about it for a few seconds and he came to the conclusion that I was backing down and he had won. He gave me a drunken wink. 'You're on.'

He gathered his two pals on either side of him and stepped back on to the pavement just as the other thirty reached the door of Crackers. 'This one's nae fuckin' good,' he roared, 'let's find another pub.' And off they went down Wardour Street, waving their scarves and scattering innocent strollers into the gutter.

Back at Crackers, the boss heaved a sigh of relief. 'That was a miracle, I don't know how to thank you, John,' he said. 'It was brilliant. You've got the security contract – every couple of years when your bloody countrymen arrive in London for their football matches! In the meantime, come here any time as a welcome guest. Anything you want is on the house.'

I helped myself to a drink. Although I hadn't won any security business from Crackers, at least I'd made a valuable contact. I still needed to get a regular contract at an established club to get a foothold in the business. But the management of Crackers weren't about to ditch their loyal Tuesday to Saturday security staff. So I had to create a new market where one didn't already exist.

'Why don't you open on a Monday?' I asked the boss. 'And then I could supply your security for at least one night a week.' He shrugged. 'It's hard enough to make ends meet on the other nights of the week. There's not enough business to justify opening on a Monday.'

'I'll do a deal with you, let *me* open the club on a Monday night. You're not using the place, let me try to make a go of it.'

He was still brimming over with gratitude after the plague of Scottish drunks had passed over the club as a result of my little miracle. 'I wouldn't have the nerve to charge you rent if you want this place on a Monday night,' he said. 'But if you think you can bring in enough customers, the club will be satisfied with the profits from the bar. And you can keep the entrance money. But I warn you, you won't make enough to cover your cab fare home.' That was it. Working undercover in Belfast I had already passed myself off as a rock 'n' roll promoter. If I could con the IRA into thinking I knew that business inside out, I could try the same tactic on the music industry itself.

Then the three Scottish soccer nuts reappeared at the door, having abandoned their compatriots to a pub-wrecking spree somewhere close to Piccadilly Circus. I ushered them up to the bar and ordered a round of free drinks, pints of very strong lager. They knocked them back and glared round the deserted club. They had proved their point, they had got inside and exerted their authority. I was happy to let them have their little moment of triumph.

'Another round, gents?' I offered.

Scarface glowered at me. 'You're fucking joking, Jimmy. We're no' hanging around this dump, it's fucking boring. We're goin' somewhere where there's a bit of life.' And they reeled out of the door. My own head was reeling slightly as well. I had my own rock club, even if it was only one night a week. It was a dizzy exhilarating feeling.

I decided to call my new Monday nightclub the Vortex. Now all I had to do was find a band to fill the place three nights later. And my luck held out spectacularly. I began phoning round ex-army buddies who were frittering away their time as club bouncers to book a couple of them for that first Monday night duty. I didn't even know if I could afford to pay them any wages for a night's work. One of the bouncers, Terry, provided the answer to all my problems. He was free that Monday because he was about to be thrown out of work. He'd been on 'guard duty' with an outrageous American band called Johnny Thunder and the Heartbreakers, one of the first punk bands.

Now, all I knew about punk was that it was an insult Edward G. Robinson used to snarl at Jimmy Cagney in bad gangster movies. Or was it Cagney to Robinson? Never mind, it didn't matter. The punk tour of the Heartbreakers had come to an abrupt end and the security staff were being paid off. The work permits for the Heartbreakers were being withdrawn by the Home Office. There were dark mutterings about drug taking, but I think it was just sheer prejudice against degenerate Yanks whose antics on stage and weird make-up made Alice Cooper look as tame as Cliff Richard. Besides the Establishment was suffering enough culture shock from our own homegrown punks who were just beginning to ooze on to the scene like a choked lavatory quietly backing up into the nation's living rooms. They figured we didn't need to import any.

So the rest of the Heartbreakers' gigs were cancelled and Terry told them he was off to work for me. Out of the blue the Heartbreakers asked him if I would agree to let them perform a farewell gig at the Vortex. And since their work permits had been revoked, they'd play for free just so they could shit on the bureaucrats at the Home Office. That was fine by me.

I then set to work on a propaganda exercise. I roped in a couple of young punks, gave them some pocket money, hoping they wouldn't spend it all on gold-plated safety-pins, and sent them off round the punk haunts to spread the word. The Heartbreakers were doing a farewell gig to spite Her Majesty the Queen and they were appearing at this shameful new Monday-night club in Wardour Street, the Vortex.

And I waited. It's a scientific fact that most punks have an attention span of ten seconds and for all I knew my spiky-haired messengers had rushed off to the nearest DIY store and were spending the weekend quietly at home with their mums and dads, gathered round the family TV and inhaling liquid Evo-Stik. If the message hadn't got around, it looked as if the opening night at the Vortex would consist of me and my staff having to pelt the Heartbreakers with beer cans and used lavatory paper, a touching ritual their doting fans were supposed to perform.

The Heartbreakers turned up, wiping their noses and other parts of their anatomies on their Home Office work-exclusion orders. And the punks eventually arrived in a suffocating mist of body odour and hair gel. It was a shambles. The total legal capacity of the premises was 650 tightly packed bodies. We crammed in more than a thousand at two pounds per head. In that first night, even after deductions for hosing the place out afterwards and disinfecting the stage, I made more money than I would have earned in three months as a sergeant in the British

Army. And I didn't have to risk a bullet in the back or a bomb under my barracks' bed.

Sure, there were some drawbacks. I felt my Scottish hackles rise when the most nauseating of the punks adopted tartan kilts worn over ripped jeans as some sort of anarchic fashion symbol. And I found myself being consulted as an agony uncle to some of the fastest-rising punk stars on the scene. They'd ask me, in all seriousness, if I thought they should wear stockings and suspenders instead of tights, or if their lipstick clashed with their eye-liner and mascara. And these were guys, for Chrissake! But my own inexperience of running a music club seemed to match exactly the raw amateurism of the new punk scene. I was supremely confident that the Vortex could handle anything that was thrown at it, that my team which included a lot of hard-bitten ex-soldiers could cope with packing the place every Monday night with the roughest, toughest, meanest punk bands in London – and their fans.

The word went out like wildfire. Punk bands so disgusting that no other club in London would touch them, were queueing up to play at the Vortex. They were so desperate to get on stage, any stage, that they pleaded to be allowed to play the Vortex – for free. They'd turn up with their own sound equipment, their own lighting, they'd play for nothing and they'd spend all week sticking up flyposters all over town advertising their appearance at the club. Within weeks I was featuring five bands every Monday night at the Vortex from 8 p.m. until three in the morning.

A lot of bands got their first break at the Vortex. I let the Sex Pistols play there to help get them the headlines and to boost the club's reputation. And then there was Generation X, with a pretty blond boy singer, Billy Idol, who was to become a good friend in later years. There were some less-memorable groups, the Buzzcocks, Enrico Cadillac, John Cooper Clark and Neo. And there was one gorgeous little Scots lass that I began to fancy for myself. She sang with the Tourists and she'd come on stage in a plastic micro-mini skirt with perfectly formed little tits poking out of her blouse. She was a cut above the normal talentless rubbish we had on stage at the Vortex and I knew she was destined for greater things. Her name was Annie Lennox.

But despite the occasional flash of real musical ability, the Vortex continued to degenerate happily into greater and greater profitability. I even began to spend some of my easy money installing a few very basic facilities. I splashed out hard cash on a permanent p.a. and sound system for the performers. I even toyed with the idea of providing dressing rooms. There were no such luxury facilities, only a curtained-off area beside the emergency stairs for the performers to get changed. The lack of privacy didn't seem to bother most of them. A quick flick back of the curtain would reveal some really appalling scenes like Billy Idol getting blow jobs from groupies, or Boy George kissing and cuddling strange men.

The sights on stage were equally astonishing. Groups like the Moors Murderers strutted about in Gestapo uniforms. In the toilets there were scenes of gross sexual depravity. I was growing tired of arguments and fights with the punks over the toilet facilities. We had conventional, segregated Ladies and Gents. But there was no way of preventing the two sexes mingling in the lavs. These punks would say to us, 'You can't tell us where to shit,' as if it was a challenge to their revolutionary way of life.

At the end of the day it was dismay at the toilet habits of my regular patrons that proved the last straw for me at the Vortex. But in the intervening months the Vortex almost grew too fast for its own good. I began to tire of the raucous punk bands and their sleazy hangers-on. I had the money to be able to afford to pay for real rock 'n' rollers, talented, respected musicians to appear on stage, and I began to get the urge to move up-market. I suppose my years of training and discipline were beginning to make me rebel against this new life-style.

I liked the money, the affluence, the new cars I could buy, the girlfriends I could wine and dine, the posh flat I had rented for myself in Fulham. I had outgrown my original slapdash approach and I was beginning to think that I could channel punk music along organised business lines and make money while still keeping my self-respect. I knew deep down inside I was in danger of becoming brutalised by the money, the noise and the squalor. With the graffiti on the walls and the filth in the unisex toilets, the place was getting to resemble a shit-stained dirty protest in the cells of the Maze Prison.

I saw the writing on the wall after a run-in with a punk group, Chelsea, who had a routinely wild stage act, and they ended up by wrecking my sound equipment. The Vortex was well past its early days as an anything-goes club. Dammit! I was now paying good money for bands to appear on stage, and I owned the sound equipment. So I told Chelsea they were barred from playing the club again and for good measure I said I'd be deducting the cost of new sound equipment from their fee. I expected a face full of spit and some wild threats. But no. They shrugged their shoulders and said their business manager would be in touch and I could expect a strongly worded letter from their lawyers. Lawyers already!

Their manager was Miles Copeland Jr, the founder of the rock group Police and sharp-witted, business-minded son of Miles Copeland Snr, the former head of the Central Intelligence Agency at the US Embassy in London. Miles knew a good thing when he saw one, even if it had a limited life span. Punk was getting to be big business and smarter guys than I who already had good contacts in the music world had seen the prospects for making really big money. Miles Copeland Jr was one of those. Malcolm McLaren was another. As manager of the Sex Pistols he was using the notoriety they had earned at the Vortex to sign them up for lucrative record deals which wouldn't have shamed legitimate rock 'n' roll stars.

Punk music wasn't really music at all and any attempt to exploit it widely on a commercial basis was going to show it up for the fleeting fraud it had been all along. I was willing to ride the gravy train myself, but I wanted to get off before it ploughed into the buffers at the end of the line. I was only amazed that it was taking so long for the rest of the music business to see through the sham. The emperors of punk had no musical ability, no clothes, their naked willies and hairy bums were on display for anyone who opened up their eyes.

I even made more money out of a privately produced album 'Live At the Vortex', featuring the most tuneless bands of our time. It must have been one of the worst records ever made, but it was hailed as a breakthrough in 'New Wave Punk'. It was all getting extremely silly.

At that stage the Americans were clamouring to get on the bandwagon of this new punk moneyspinner. They seemed to think that anything that was sweeping England was bound to set the States alight just as the Beatles and Rolling Stones had done a decade earlier. Producers and distributors were flocking in from the States. They couldn't believe their eyes or their ears but they were still opening up their cheque books and hoping for the best.

But there was one sharp music-business executive who wasn't taken in by the hype. He could see quite clearly that this particular balloon was going to burst with a loud farting noise and go whizzing round in circles until it vanished up its own raucous arse. This executive, the UK head of an American Record label, was hosting the annual conference of all his American top talent scouts. They had been flown in from the States and they were living it up in the swanky Grosvenor Hotel. Our executive didn't get where he was by not checking out new trends and spotting winners in advance, so he spent many a Monday night at the Vortex. He'd been under a lot of pressure from the States to get in on the ground floor and sign up some of these headline-making new British punks. He had signed up a few of them but he wasn't too sure if his company bosses back home knew what he was up against.

So he came along to the Vortex a few times and now he wanted to do a deal with me to show his American scouts exactly what British punk was all about; he didn't want any of them being overwhelmed and baffled by the atmosphere and blowing his company money signing up lavatory attendants and glue-sniffers to five-year exclusive contracts as the new Johnny Rotten.

He turned up a week in advance and stood in the corner in his snazzy Brooks Brothers suit and watched a succession of bands doing their best, or their worst. Later we had a drink in my private office. 'My God, John,' he laughed. 'That stuff is absolute crap. It's junk. How much longer are these truly awful people going to get away with this?'

I was defensive. 'It's definitely the stuff for the younger generation. The likes of you and I might find it a little . . . er . . . unusual . . . at first, but it takes a little while for all real musical pioneers to be recognised for an original breakthrough. You're looking at potential superstars who could be keeping your record label on top if you sign them up right now while you've got the chance.'

He squared up to me, man to man, and stared deeply into my eyes. Then he put his arms around me in a bear hug and slapped me violently on the back. 'You son-of-a-bitch! Never try to play poker against me. I could just see it in your face, I could just smell it! It's all baloney and shit and you know it. These people are going nowhere!'

There was no way out. I smiled weakly and admitted: 'You're dead right. But I'll swear on a stack of Bibles I've never admitted this to you.'

He roared with laughter. 'John, this is absolutely wonnerful! It's the discovery I've been looking for. I want you to do me a real favour. I want to rent the Vortex for the night, next Monday, private party. Name your price. I want you to showcase some of our new bands on stage. Some of the people we've been giving contracts to. Yeah, and some of their fans to give the place the right atmosphere.'

In the privacy of my office we did the deal. And I listened carefully to what he had in mind. An hour later I went on stage and announced the bad news that the Vortex would be closed to the public the following Monday. A private party, I explained, dodging a hail of beer cans. Then I announced the good news. There would be complimentary tickets for selected regulars. I gave my trusty lieutenants Fred and Terry a wad of about five hundred tickets as freebies for the next Monday. And I told them exactly what kind of regular customer should have the privilege of getting a comp ticket.

The following afternoon the caterers arrived at the Vortex and spread out £3,000 of pâté de foie gras and barbecued chicken and fine wines and sophisticated German beers. By mid-evening the place was packed with the carefully selected customers who had been given the freebie tickets. At 11 p.m. the fleet of limos arrived from the Grosvenor, bearing the cream of the record company wheeler-dealers. These guys weren't all naïve Bible-belt bigots. They included big boys from LA and New York, Chicago and Miami. Admittedly a lot of them were wearing polyester slacks with white shoes and short-sleeved shirts. But given the law of averages, I suppose at least some of them had seen service in Vietnam.

A particularly loud and raucous punk group were on stage. And this big guy from Philadelphia, all Rayban sunglasses and capped teeth, tapped one of the little girls on the shoulder and said: 'Hi, I'm Al, who's this interesting new band?'

She spun round and snapped at him: 'Don't you fucking Americans know anything?'

He stepped back into a bank of strobe lights and stuttered apologetically: 'Now listen, little girl, I was just trying to be friendly.' She smiled. 'Well, that's OK then.' And with a clatter of safety-pins and chains and spiked dog-collars, she took a running jump and locked her legs round Al's waist and gave him a big wet kiss on the mouth. There was a burst of bright strobe light and Al saw she was wearing a used tampon as an ear-ring. And he nearly passed out.

The evening was downhill after that. Men who braved the crowd to get close to the stage to try to discern any rhythm in the music, got caught up in the hail of spit, gob and chicken legs which weren't aimed at anybody in particular. Another American went into the toilets and was so overcome by the stench and the puddles of stale beer that he brought up the remains of his buffet dinner all over his white sports jacket. As he lurched back into the mêlée, one of the fans of Wayne County and the Electric Chairs, green snot dripping from his nose, saw the trail of vomit down the guy's jacket, handed him a half-empty can of beer and said cheerfully: 'Getting into the mood, mate? Fuckin' good here, innit?'

The record men who had flown the Atlantic hoping to leapfrog the company promotion ladder by making the musical discoveries of the decade, were falling by the wayside, claiming headaches and blackouts and calling for their limos. All in all, the evening was a great success.

Their boss was delighted. It meant an end to all that hassle about signing up more and more punks. He wasn't going to sign up anyone unless he thought theywere worth it. Just to be on the safe side he gave me his private phone number and said: 'If you come across the new answer to the Beatles, get them under contract and bring them straight to me. In the meantime I think my fellow Americans will be content with getting back home and trying to spot in advance who's going to be the next John Denver.'

The Vortex was already past its peak, but it still had the reputation of being the biggest punk club in all of Europe. Such was our fame, or infamy, that I could charge £100 a time 'facility fee' for allowing cameramen inside to film the scenes for syndication around the world to TV stations who wanted to show their viewers the new British disease.

One cameraman was Martin Baker, the son of film star Stanley Baker. Martin was making a documentary. He had paid his money and he was shooting uninterrupted footage of a band called the Slits, when a girl got up on stage, lifted her skirt, squatted down and had a piss right there and then. It was the routine kind of stunt some bands pulled when they wanted to get the audience's undivided attention. My only concern was that the stream of piss might short circuit some of the electrics and she'd get a high-voltage spark where it would really hurt and ruin her chances of motherhood.

Martin Baker was livid. 'John,' he complained above the wild applause, 'that's so disgusting. It's ruined my film. It's too far over the top, I'll never be able to sell this anywhere. I want my money back.'

The refund was going to be no problem. But I didn't want Martin as a dissatisfied customer. And I was getting annoyed that this sort of behaviour was becoming more frequent and more irritating, as well as messy and unhygienic. So I yelled at my main bouncer Freddie Prime: 'Fred, kindly escort that young lady from the premises!'

Fred forced a path through the cheering punks, got on stage and just lifted her up and pinned her under one of his massive arms. He came striding through the club with her and I waited by the front door to open it for him. Before they reached me, the girl jerked her head round to one side and sank her teeth into Freddie's hand, drawing blood. It was gut reaction. Freddie lifted his free hand and whacked her across the face. And she went unconscious. We got her to the front door and we were both worried that Freddie had broken her jaw, or maybe even broken her neck. But after a minute or two she came round. She got unsteadily to her feet and spat straight into Freddie's face.

We looked at each other, both trained Guardsmen who had fought together in Malaya, and I wondered if I really wanted to run a punk club or if Freddie really should be earning a living smacking silly little girls unconscious.

So I gave up the Vortex club and formed Executive Security.

<u>Biggs</u>

I've nothing personal against Ronnie Biggs. I had to snatch him, or abduct him, or kidnap him, take your choice, for the same reason that climbers risk everything to get to the top of Everest. Because he was there.

Ronnie was just another second-class villain among the gang who ambushed the Glasgow to London overnight mail train on a deserted stretch of track forty miles north of London in August 1963 at the same time as I was a teenage trainee at the Guards' depot in Pirbright. The Great Train Robbery was world-wide headlines and a lot of the ordinary British public didn't make too much of a secret about having at least some sneaking admiration for the robbery gang. The gang had cracked the driver over the head but at least they hadn't killed anybody. And they made off with £2,631,784. It ranked as a world-record robbery and gave British crooks a lot of prestige in international crime circles.

Like everyone else in Britain, I was intrigued to read the newspaper reports of the train raid. 'The robbery was carried out with military precision', the papers were saying and I had a good laugh at that: military precision – polished boots and buttons and train robbery by numbers. All that happened was that members of the gang just did the jobs they had been given without getting lost in the dark. A little bit of co-ordination and nerve goes into a crime and the press starts raving about 'military precision'. At the end of the day everybody who didn't deserve it got a good result. The crooks won a lot of public notoriety and even managed to hold on to about £2 million of the loot. Scotland Yard rounded a lot of them up. There were promotions for the top brass who never left their offices and Masonic clubs and lots of lovely overtime for the CID plodders who hung around the pubs long enough to buy the right information on who was suddenly rich. A few months' later it was pay-day for solicitors and barristers at the show trial and finally it was the turn of the Establishment who got a big kick out of the thirty-year sentences dished out to the gang.

Then Ronnie upset the scales of justice. He served less than two years of his stretch in Wandsworth Prison, South London. At 3.10 p.m. on Thursday, 8 July 1965, a masked face popped above the top of the prison wall, a rope ladder was thrown over, and Ronnie and three other cons shinned up, jumped into a getaway car, switched to a series of other vehicles and safe houses and got clean away.

By this time I was a fully fledged Guardsman, on public duty outside Buckingham Palace, looking at the world with tunnel vision through the archway of a sentry-box. I read the newspaper reports next day. The jail break, they said, was carried out with, you've guessed it, 'military precision'. It was just a passing thought, but I wondered why nobody considered using 'military precision' to take out these great criminal tacticians who the press were convinced were the masterminds behind every bank and jewellery heist in Britain. What about putting the Flying Squad on guard duty outside Buckingham Palace, truncheons and whistles gleaming, and getting a battalion of Guards or Paras to clean up gangland?

Ronnie wasn't back in the news for nearly ten years after his jail break. Then from his bolt-hole in Brazil he made contact with a reporter from the *Daily Express*.

Ronnie was broke and he did a deal for £35,000 to sell his story of a decade on the run. And he wanted the reporter to sound out his chances of serving a shorter sentence if he gave himself up. While Ronnie thought the *Daily Express* were looking after his best interests the paper craftily tipped off Scotland Yard and Detective Chief Superintendent Jack Slipper flew to Rio, promptly arrested Ronnie and tried to fly him back to London. But this operation had been planned and executed with 'Scotland Yard precision'. The Brazilians didn't take to being railroaded by bossy British detectives. There were a series of comic opera court appearances in the Supreme Court in Brasilia and Biggs was allowed to stay in Brazil, almost a free man.

Ronnie boasted he had been saved by the power of his prick. Banged up in a Brazilian jail while his lawyers argued with Scotland Yard, one of his cellmates asked him: 'Got a Brazilian girlfriend?' He told Ronnie quite casually about Law 941 of the Brazilian Code of Justice, which says that the parent of a Brazilian kid can't be extradited. After all the money Ronnie had paid out for minders, safe houses, plastic surgery and fake passports, he got the best piece of aiding and abetting he'd ever got in his life. And it was free.

The cellmate was a streetwise Rio cabbie called Mario who said: 'If you've got ready cash get your girlfriend straight down to a maternity hospital to buy a baby. There are plenty of new mothers in Rio who'll sell their babies for a few dollars.' But Ronnie was stony broke. 'OK,' said Mario. 'If you've not got the money for a ready-made kid straight from the factory, as it were, get a girlfriend to say she's pregnant. That'll give you a breathing space for a few months, seven or eight if you push it.'

Ronnie was living with a nineteen-year-old samba dancer called Lucia who looked after her waistline and who'd been interviewed and posed for *Daily Express* photographs. And it was obvious from her figure she wasn't sacrificing her dancing career to give birth to a little Train Robber. But Ronnie had been knocking off a whole string of bar girls, and one of them, Raimunda, a nightclub stripper he had ditched the year before, coincidentally decided the day after she visited him in jail at Praca Quinze, that she was already pregnant and having his baby. She produced a son seven months after Biggs had been arrested. Biggs was allowed to stay in Brazil on Conditional Liberty, with the only restrictions that he had to reside at a fixed address and sign the register at a Rio police station twice a week. It was a damned sight better than going back to London in hand-cuffs to finish a thirty-year stretch in Wandsworth.

The whole episode was something of a farce, with Jack Slipper cast in the starring role of 'Superintendent Clouseau goes to Rio' and Ronnie, who was just a randy, homesick failed crook, trying to convince everybody he was a master criminal who had outwitted justice once again. It was a lucky escape for Ronnie and he should have done a lot of silent praying. But then he never did have any sense. He didn't know when to keep a low profile and from then on he rubbed their noses in it. He'd sell off newspaper and magazine interviews every few months. If a tourist bought a souvenir 'I've met Ronnie Biggs' T-shirt, he'd only charge them a few extra cruzeiros to pose with them for a photo on the beach to impress the folks back home. He was really going over the top.

He even dropped the Royal Navy in the shit. One weekend when he had been to sign on at the police station, Ronnie spotted a couple of Navy ratings shopping in a beach-side market. Always ready to scrounge money for a souvenir picture or an autograph, he introduced himself. The sailors were from H M S *Danae*, a Royal Navy warship on manoeuvres with the Brazilians and moored in Rio harbour. The drinks flowed and Ronnie wangled himself an invitation aboard the *Danae* where he guzzled plenty of Her Majesty's booze in the mess before the officer of the watch discovered he was on board and booted him off.

If only the duty officer had quietly banged Ronnie up in the brig and set sail with him muffled and in chains, he could have saved us all a lot of trouble. Ronnie managed to liberate some English tea and Colman's mustard from the sympathetic sailors before he was landed back on the dockside. He repaid their hospitality by inviting a couple of them back to his house, where he set them up for a party witnessed by a reporter friend who sold the story to Fleet Street and split the proceeds with Biggs.

He was at it again a couple of years later when my former Vortex stars, the Sex Pistols, turned up in Rio and offered Ronnie some money to cut a disc with them. As an extra bit of blasphemy and hype, they hired a church in Rio for the recording where a very drunken Ronnie joined in the tuneless renderings of 'God Save Martin Bormann' and 'Belsen was a Gas'.

It was obvious by this time that he'd do anything for a few quid and I think any sympathy that people had left for him back home in Britain had turned to annoyance and disgust. But, as I said, I've nothing personal against Biggs and I wasn't giving it much thought when I was sitting brooding in my new office above a strip club in Soho. It was 1979, two years after I had left the Army and a year after I had given up the Vortex club. The company I had formed, Executive Security, was meant to bring real 'military precision' within the reach of anyone with a lot of money to throw around.

The brochure for prospective clients said it all: Governments toppled, estimates free. Revolutions and uprisings organised, armed struggles orchestrated, terrorism ruthlessly suppressed. No job too big, no job too small. Distance no object. Easy payments arranged, special discounts for repeat customers. Problem was, the CIA and the KGB and MI6 already had most of the business sewn up and they could afford better credit terms than I could. If your government's face fitted, they'd do it for free and as a bonus they'd credit your Swiss bank account with a contribution to the unofficial presidential pension fund.

Executive Security had only one client at that time, Baron Stephen Bentinck. Stephen is the nephew of German steel millionaire, Baron Heine Thyssen. The Thyssens had been having some problems with the Baader-Meinhof left-wing terrorists who were pretty active in the kidnap, ransom and murder racket and I basically ran a bodyguard and intelligence service for the British branch of the family. My office in Greek Street was the size of a cupboard but it was provided free by Stephen because it also served as the mailing address for a defunct movie company he owned called Legion Films. Stephen wasn't one of the heavy industry Thyssens, the old Teutonic dynasty who had joined forces with the Krupps to help Hitler to power. He was in the entertainments business, dabbling in restaurants and publishing. He knew me through our mutual showbiz connections. He wouldn't have been a great political catch for the Baader-Meinhof group. Cabinet ministers wouldn't have been wakened in the middle of the night to be told the news. But he was family, and he was vulnerable.

The contract with him brought in enough money for me to keep a couple of old army buddies on the payroll. Freddie Prime had loyally followed me from the Vortex. And I'd hired Norrie Boyle who had recovered from being blown up in Belfast, and who'd decided he was all washed up with the Army. Executive Security wasn't toppling any governments, it was just working on trying to build a track record, however modest, in the hope that the big break was just around the corner. That means it was paying its phone bill and its bar bill and that's a good start.

But it was hard to look on the contract with Stephen as more than just a training exercise. He wouldn't take my advice about his personal security seriously and he'd slip away any chance he got for a night's partying. So I'd send Freddie Prime after him. Stephen would come lurching out of a restaurant or club, oblivious to everything except the girlfriend on his arm and Freddie would pounce on him from a darkened doorway and shout, 'Boo', in what Fred thought was a menacing German accent. Or Stephen would leave his car in a public parking lot and get back to find the lock had been picked and a visiting card from Executive Security taped over the ignition lock just where the detonating wire would have run to a bomb under the driver's seat. It should have been a serious cat and mouse game with some real risks and some real penalties. But it was just like a Tom and Jerry caper where a stick of cartoon TNT would explode in the mousetrap, we'd all get our whiskers and furry arses blown off and turn up in the next frame as if nothing had happened.

I think Stephen would have let this Warner Bros scenario go on for ever. He could afford it. But I thought it was time to get back into the real world, even if it meant putting an end to the regular pay cheque. I told him Executive Security would carry out a pre-emptive strike. We'd figure out a way of going to Germany and getting alongside Baader-Meinhof and sort the problem out at source. Apart from the comic cuts capers with Stephen, I'd done some serious research on Baader-Meinhof. They were a reasonably dangerous bunch, but not as professional as they were cracked up to be. They had their share of slipshod cockups and poor security, the Kraut Factor, just like my old friends in the Provisional IRA suffered from the Mick Factor.

It was no good, Stephen didn't want to take the fight to the enemy camp. Well, were there any foreign regimes he wanted overthrown? Maybe just a shaky dictatorship already so near the brink that it would only take Freddie, Norrie and me to knock them over and get in some practice before moving on to bigger prestige contracts like Angola or Libya. The Thyssen family didn't want to know.

I had to be honest with Stephen. I was ready to step off the gravy train and give up the rent-free office. After a while I confessed to him: 'You'd better know there's no way I could stop a really determined kidnapper getting his hands on you. Doesn't matter how well hidden you are, how many guards you've got round you, there's nobody who can't be captured if the kidnappers have got the right motivation.'

He wasn't happy about this. 'Maybe I should switch my security, John,' he challenged me.

I would have welcomed that. 'I'll make a bet with you Stephen,' I countered. 'Get another security outfit and we'll have their set-up penetrated in less than a month and we could snatch you any time after that. I've already had to work out how to do that because if you want to learn how to prevent somebody being kidnapped, the first thing you've got to do is think like a kidnapper and work out every possible combination of pulling off a successful kidnap. I could pick out a target now and work out a capture plan.'

I listened to what I was saying. Shit! Pull off a success-ful snatch of a VIP, where they didn't come to any harm, and Executive Security would have clients beating a path to its door.

'Stephen,' I said. 'I'll show you what I mean. You put up the money and I'll snatch somebody as a feasibility exercise. We'll be internationally famous, or notorious, overnight, and you can be the major shareholder in a private army of go-anywhere do-anything mercenary Supermen.'

In many ways Stephen was a bored rich kid. And the idea appealed to him. But he quite naturally came up with the logical, practical, legal and moral objection. 'Christ, John,' he argued. 'You just can't go out and kidnap somebody because it's good publicity for your business.'

'No, no . . .' I was speaking as fast as the idea was forming. 'Not kidnap . . . uhh . . . snatch . . . uhh . . . capture, no . . . arrest. That's it *arrest* people who can't be touched by the conventional forces of law and order . . .'

'You're mad! Arrest who, for Christ's sake? You gonna set yourself up as judge and bloody jury and executioner?'

'No, no. People who have already been judged guilty but have got away with it.' I paused, desperate to pluck an example from thin air. 'Like . . . like Josef Mengele . . . Martin Bormann.' I thought for a second I'd blown it. Maybe asking the Thyssens for finance to capture Nazi war criminals was about as tactful as asking the Mafia for the dough to find Jimmy Hoffa's killer. It didn't seem to bother Stephen. He went quiet. 'Jeez, John, that's big.'

'Or . . . Lord Lucan, yeah, Lord Lucan. He's been missing for years now since his nanny was battered to death. Nobody knows if he's alive or dead. The coroner's court has already declared him a murderer, just nobody can find him.'

'Yeah, yeah, he's a good one.' Stephen was reaching for his cheque book. And as an afterthought I added: 'Or that arrogant cockney train robbing bastard in Brazil, what's his name . . . Ronnie . . . Ronnie Biggs.'

It didn't take much careful consideration to decide that Ronnie was the favourite after all. Sure, he wasn't in the same league as Mengele or Bormann or 'Lucky' Lucan, the aristocratic gambler. But more of him later. Ronnie Biggs was definitely the right target to get our new enterprise off the ground. At least we knew, or could find out from friendly sources, exactly what was his current address in Rio.

Within a couple of days I had started to sketch out a

rough plan. It would mean a yacht, probably to and from the island of Antigua, one of the nearest old British colonial islands to the coast of Brazil and an easy place to charter a boat with no questions asked. I reckoned I'd need an executive jet too. And there'd be hotel and 'entertainment' expenses. 'Time spent on reconnaissance is seldom wasted.' That was the army dictum. I agreed.

I enjoyed setting it all up. It was going to be an all-Guards production with me and my old friends Fred and Norrie. I had a ready-made alias. The name 'Chris Demetriou' appeared on the headed notepaper of Legion Films as a co-director with Stephen Bentinck. I invented a new persona for him, as a slick, wheeler-dealer Anglo Greek Cypriot.

We built up a whole high-powered image for Chris Demetriou. The phone would go and the caller would ask to speak to Chris Demetriou and Fred or Norrie would say 'Mr Demetriou is in a business conference' or 'He's flying back from Geneva later today, can he get back to you?' I worked on the kind of Greek accent you find around the kebab houses and gambling joints of Soho, and opened a modest Swiss bank account in Demetriou's name. There was the headed notepaper and the well-established office address of Stephen's movie company. It was very smart writing paper from a good show-business address and letters on it from Chris Demetriou, Executive Producer, impressed the hell out of people.

That was how we made the booking to hire the executive Lear jet. There was no way they'd have rented a Lear jet to an ex-Guards sergeant operating from a single room in Soho. But to a film producer with a fancy Greek name and a Swiss bank account? No problem. But before we got into all the smart stuff like chartering yachts and jets, there was a whole lot of basic research to do. Assembling a dossier on Biggs wasn't difficult. As I've said he took every chance to flaunt himself and the newspaper clippings were full of details of the apartment where he lived and the beach bars where he hung out.

There were also reports of the biggest excitement in Rio, short of Carnival. Roger Moore had been in town with the whole James Bond crew shooting scenes for the *Moonraker* movie. It only took a short visit, a couple of streets away, to the London office of Cubby Broccoli, the executive producer of the Bond movies, carefully scheduled at lunch-time when most of the bosses were munching and drinking their way through expense accounts. I chatted up the receptionist while Freddie did a clean sweep of a couple of desktops and we left with a briefcase full of *Moonraker* promo and production papers, all with the 007 logo. Then, a drink with a friend who ran a quick-print shop in Soho and I had enough beautifully counterfeit James Bond headed paper to write my own movie shooting schedule.

A check call to a contact at Scotland Yard and I had an approved list of the nearest Caribbean islands to Brazil which had automatic extradition treaties with Britain. Antigua, where I planned to hire the yacht, looked like the best bet for landing Ronnie. If I could lure Ronnie eighteen hundred miles from Rio to Belem, the port on Brazil's northern coast, we could sail straight into international waters and head for the island.

Before long the little office in Soho was plastered with maps of South and Central America. As far as Brazil itself was concerned, we treated it much like Belfast, hostile territory. We invested in a set of large-scale maps of Rio and particularly of the neighbourhood where Ronnie was living. We marked all the courthouses, police stations and government offices. We had to be one hundred per cent certain about where the police threat would be. We checked everything. We looked at Ronnie's house and his neighbours' houses. We went over those maps time and time again. It's why marathon runners or show jumpers or golfers like to walk the course before they go out and do it for real. It gives you confidence if you know the terrain backwards.

Renting a boat to sail the two thousand miles between Belem and Antigua was a case for Chris Demetriou. It's not as simple as hiring a car from Hertz or Avis. Owners are inclined to be neurotic about letting just anybody sail away on half-a-million-pounds-worth of yacht. They tend to ask awkward questions. Naturally we went to the top because we wanted the best boat possible. In the world of yacht hire, or chartering to use the business term, the top people are Nicholsons. They do for boats what Owen and Owen do for anyone who wants a Rolls-Royce for the weekend. I went to their London office, wearing my best suit, flashed my Legion Films business card and told the posh salesman that we were filming in Rio and planned to take a sailing holiday immediately afterwards. He was visibly impressed, got out all the brochures and after a happy half hour we had shaken hands on a deal to charter a black, wooden-hulled, six-berth, Italian-built seventy-two footer called the *Ocean Scorpion*. She was moored in Antigua, skippered by an Englishman named Steve Adamson, who was assisted by his wife and a crewman called Bobby Ingles. The deal was that Steve would sail her down to Belem, pick up four people and sail back to Antigua. I chartered her for three weeks at 10,000 dollars a week.

Once that was settled I decided the time had come to survey the lie of the land at first hand and for real. As I checked in at Heathrow for the Varig flight to Rio, I couldn't help reflecting that the last time anyone had tried such an outrageous snatch of a fugitive was when Mossad, the Israeli intelligence agency, had spirited Adolf Eichmann out of Argentina in 1960. They had all the resources of the State of Israel at their disposal. I had Fred, Norrie and £50,000. Not that I'm disparaging Fred or Norrie. After all Fred is a tough character. He was once in an army boxing tournament in Kenya when he came up against a mean, powerful hulk who was a Regimental Sergeant Major in the King's African Rifle. Fred squared up to the RSM and gave him a real going over before knocking him out cold. The RSM was Idi Amin who became dictator of Uganda. So Fred is a useful man to have with you if you get into a fight. Problem is, if Fred isn't with you, you'd never get into a fight in the first place. But this really was a shoestring operation. The only comfort I could get out of comparing our resources with those of Mossad was that the Scots are meaner than the Jews so the budget would probably be enough.

Norrie Boyle flew in with me for the recce and we checked into a hotel on the Isla de Gobernado – Governor's Island. The Sunshine Hotel turned out to be a house of assignation, full of middle-aged businessmen bonking their secretaries, but it was a good base, and we were soon able to case Ronnie's house and hangouts. The cover story for Norrie and me was that we were a couple of stuntmen, stragglers left over from the *Moonraker* film crew. We spent the first few days soaking up the sunshine and local geography.

It was after a week that I had a real stroke of luck in the shapely form of a beautiful Brazilian girl called Elli. I bumped into her at the friendly hamburger stand on the beach opposite the hotel and it wasn't long before we were the love of each other's lives. That first weekend at her aunt's beach house I discovered, in one of our rare bursts of conversation, that Elli's father, Jose, was a policeman. And not just any old policeman, but a '*delegado*', which meant he ran a police district. And not just any old '*delegacia*' or district, but the one Ronnie Biggs lived in.

I didn't get to meet Elli's father until the following weekend. I think she was a little surprised by my eagerness to meet the family when we could have been enjoying each other's company. It was tantalising. I waited for hours as we drank beer and made small talk. But finally Jose, the *delegado*, said what I had been hoping for. 'We have a very famous Englishman in Rio.'

'Oh, yeah. Who's that then?' I was trying to sound very casual.

'Ronnie Biggs.' Elli's dad sounded really proud to have him on his patch. I took a nonchalant sip of the local brew.

'Ronnie who?'

'Biggs, the Great Train Robber. Every Wednesday and Friday at noon he comes to my police station to sign the register. It is a condition of his stay here.' What a break! Talk about mixing business with pleasure.

Ronnie's compulsory 'probationary' visits to the police station were just petty restrictions placed on him as a sop to national pride and bureaucracy. Ronnie had entered Brazil on a forged passport and they wanted to let him know, in their own way, that they still held his fate in their hands and he had better not embarrass them again. Now, because I had become a family friend of Jose, I had a ready-made excuse for hanging about the *delegacia* without arousing suspicion.

Next Wednesday, Norrie and I took up a position in a convenient bar opposite Jose's *delegacia*. It was a fine sunny morning and before long Ronnie breezed into sight, looking tanned and fit with grey hair down over his collar. Ten minutes later he came out of the police station and headed off down to the beach. We tailed him at a discreet distance and when he ambled into a bar we kept on walking. I wanted to see him for myself. I wanted to encounter and identify our target. For a middle-aged guy he looked able to handle himself. And, of course, as a villain living on the run, he probably still had fast enough reflexes to start lashing out with his fists or any handy weapons if he sensed any threat of capture. He could put up enough struggle in a restaurant or out in the street to

122

bring the whole Rio police force down around our ears. As Norrie and I flew back to London to put the final phase of the Biggs snatch into operation, I decided the best way to capture the Great Train Robber was with an offer of money and then some gentle persuasion.

Back in Britain there were two last-minute items I had to attend to. Fred and I went to a bar near the Guards' depot at Chelsea Barracks and met a couple of army friends who had visited the depot stores and 'borrowed' a marquee valise, a strong canvas bag about six feet long, fitted with four carrying handles and normally used for transporting heavy canvas marquee tents to be erected in the field. It can also be used to hold a man weighing up to two hundred pounds.

And there was the small matter of arranging world-wide publicity to break in the headlines immediately after the snatch. For that I went to Scotland to visit my old mate Gavin Goodwin, a reporter with the *Sunday Mail* in Glasgow. I'd once briefly worked for him as a photo-grapher when he ran a little press agency in Motherwell. Gavin, like so many journalists, was always going on about 'the big break'. Woodward and Bernstein were second-rate as far as he was concerned. They'd just got the break when they stumbled across the Watergate affair. So when I was right into this Biggs business, I thought to myself I'll do Gavin a favour. It's going to be a big press story anyway. I'll make sure my friend Gavin gets first crack at it and is covered in glory. It might have seemed odd to let a local paper in Scotland have the exclusive tip-off on the story, but I'm nothing if not a patriotic Jock. It was a Scots Guard operation after all. And anyway the *Sunday Mail* is owned by the *Mirror* Group in London so I was giving a fellow Scot the chance to rub his English bosses' noses in it while I still had the reassurance that he could call on the resources of a big national newspaper group to cover the story.

A few days later all three of us, myself and Norrie and Fred, flew out to Rio. We weren't going to waste any time on this trip. When we arrived I allowed my 'team' a day's rest while I showed up at Santos Dumont Airport in Rio. Santos Dumont is the internal airport for flights within Brazilian borders, no hassle with customs or immigration. I flashed the Legion Films receipt for the chartered Lear jet, they confirmed the money had been received weeks earlier from the account of Chris Demetriou, and I told them I would give them twenty-four hours' notice to put the jet on standby.

Then it was time to rig our first face-to-face meeting with Ronnie Biggs. It was just before midday when we cruised past the bar in Sepetiba in Rio's southern suburbs, where we knew he always went for his first heart-starting drink of the day. He was there all right, sitting on a stool in the shadow just inside the bar, knocking back a cold beer. I swung the car into the side of the road and made a big play of opening the bonnet. With an oily rag round my hand I loosened off the radiator cap and let out a loud curse in English as a cloud of steam jetted out from the engine. As Fred and Norrie got out of the car, cursing equally loudly, Ronnie heard the commotion and came wandering out of the bar to join in the fun. 'I live just down the street,' he volunteered. 'Buy me a beer and I'll get you a jug with water for your motor.'

Within fifteen minutes of meeting Ronnie Biggs we were inside his house. It was all going like a dream, I was spinning Ronnie a yarn about being a movie director shooting some extra James Bond footage, Fred was trying to chat up Ronnie's latest live-in girlfriend Ulla. Then little Mike Biggs arrived. And the whole plan nearly started to come unstuck. It's not true what they say about Guardsmen eating babies for breakfast. We actually have a soft spot for kids. Little Mike was five years old with that cute, dark South American Indian look about him. Norrie was bouncing him up and down on his knee. I had to get us out of there.

We went back to the car with the water jug, I spilled most of the water over the engine block, replaced the radiator cap and took Ronnie back into the bar for another beer.

'You've done us a great favour, Ronnie,' I told him. 'I had to get that car running because I'm due back at the Copacabana Hotel to make a phone call to Lewis Gilbert who's been directing the Bond movie. I'll try to return the favour. I'll see if I can wangle some work in the movie for you.'

Ronnie got straight to the point. 'Will there be some dough in it for me?'

'Sure, sure. I'll see what I can do. Come up to the Copacabana the day after tomorrow and I'll phone Lewis. Bring little Mike with you and we'll make it a day out.'

Ronnie grunted: 'I've got to sign on at the nick on Friday so that's fine for me, but I'll leave the kid here, I don't want him trailing along.'

'Hey, he's your son, Ronnie, he'd like a day out with his old man.'

Ronnie ordered another beer on my tab and volunteered: 'I'm not his old man and he's not my son. He's my residence permit, but that's a long story, John.' Suddenly I felt a lot better, a lot cleaner, and a lot more ready to see this through.

The psychology for getting Ronnie in our clutches wasn't going to be complex. He wasn't a very complex man. I'd just use a variation of the trick the black garden boy had taught me all those years ago in Rhodesia. When the garden boy and I went into the bush, we caught monkeys by getting a clear glass bottle with a small neck and putting some fruit in it. Then we'd tie the bottle to a tree. The monkey would see the bait, put his hand in greedily and grab the fruit. It wouldn't have the sense to let go and its clenched fist was too big to bring back through the neck of the bottle. That way you'd catch your monkey. It was a valuable lesson. Even the most smartass monkey could be trapped by just a moment of curiosity, greed and panic. And I figured Ronnie Biggs would show all the instincts of a monkey if he got a clenched fist round a bundle of cash.

The scene at the Copacabana Hotel that Friday couldn't have gone better. Ronnie arrived and almost dived head first into the drinks cabinet of my suite on the second floor. I began to outline the fake movie deal. The whole James Bond *Moonraker* circus had finished filming and moved on, I explained to Ronnie. He already knew that. But there was still a chance of him earning some fast money for a cameo role in the movie. Ronnie had actually been offered a small spot in the movie when the crew were in Rio shooting. I already knew that. He would have jumped at the chance, but the star, Roger Moore, the son of an honest London bobby, refused to allow it. He didn't want to glorify or flatter the Train Robber. Still, ours was a plausible story and Ronnie bought it.

Our hotel room was littered with 007 fake shooting schedules and I soon convinced Biggs I was the director of a second unit still filming back-up scenes in Brazil. I told him the walkie-talkies lying on the bed, which we would have used to co-ordinate the snatch, were for camera direction, and there was still a part in the movie for Ronnie. It was a simple scene. Two of the movie's bad guys were on a sleek black 72-foot yacht, the *Ocean Scorpion*, discussing how to neutralise James Bond, while, in the background, Ronnie Biggs relaxed on deck with each arm round a busty Brazilian girl. Ronnie would have one line of dialogue: 'If James Bond is as clever as Scotland Yard, you'll have no problems.'

Ronnie loved it. And his mouth was watering at the prospect of the $10,000 I had promised him in cash. The only problem, I explained to Ronnie, was that since our Bond film crew had wrapped up in Rio, he had to fly with us to Belem to film the yacht scene.

'Shit, I can't do it,' Ronnie moaned. 'I'm not allowed to leave the Rio district. It's part of my probation. Can you shift the yacht down here to Rio and I'll do the business there?'

'No way, Ronnie,' I told him, 'we've got deadlines and schedules to meet. Pity about that, it's really just an overnight trip to Belem and back. Still, easy come, easy go.' I slipped open a desk drawer and pulled out a glossy folder with the 007 logo stamped across the top. I opened the folder slowly, making sure Ronnie could see the bundle of banknotes inside, about fifteen thousand dollars, all that was left of our budget. I pulled out a wad of money, it looked like about ten thousand dollars, and turned to Fred. 'Fred, take this downstairs to the manager's office and get him to lock it up in the safe. In the morning I want you to get straight down to the Banco de Brasil and pay this into Cubby Broccoli's Number Two Expenses Account. No point in having this dough lying around if we are not going to pay it out to Ronnie. Better get it straight back into the bank before we are tempted to dip into it. You know what that mean bastard Broccoli is like about having to account for every cent.'

Ronnie's eyes were bulging out of their sockets. He reached out and clamped my wrist as I tried to pass the money to Fred. He had the strong, desperate grip of a man who can't bear to see money slipping away from him. 'Wait, John, don't be in such a hurry, I might find a way of doing this after all.'

I glared at him. 'Ronnie, if you can't meet the deadlines, then don't piss me about.'

'No, no. There's a way I can do it. Leave it for a week, until next Friday. I sign on at the *delegacia* at twelve and then I'm not expected back until the following

Wednesday. That gives me plenty of time to get up to Belem with you and back before anyone knows I've gone.'

'What? And drop me and the boys in the shit because you've broken your probation. No way, Ronnie. Broccoli and Lewis Gilbert would fire us on the spot. I'm not laying our jobs on the line just because you want to earn a quick ten thousand bucks.'

'Listen, John, nobody would ever know I'd left town for a couple of days, I swear it.'

'What about your kid, Mike? You can't go bringing him along.'

'He's no problem. I just get a baby-sitter in to look after him. I do that all the time. I've got a black chick who lives down near the beach and I'm always spending the night with her. Mikie and the neighbours are used to me staying away from home for a couple of nights at a time. It's just that I've never slipped out of town before, but that doesn't matter.'

I was hesitating. 'I don't know, Ronnie, it all sounds too risky to me. I don't want you getting into trouble and I don't want to get the boys fired or banged up in jail for aiding and abetting you.'

Ronnie was pleading. 'Tell you what, John, I'll do a deal. Let me just do this part in the film and you and the boys can split three grand between you. I'll sign a receipt for your boss saying I got the whole ten grand and you and Fred and Norrie can have three of that for yourselves.'

I looked at Fred and Norrie and they were slowly nodding agreement, not rushing it, just looking that little bit uncertain about taking a bribe from a Great Train Robber. It was time for me to exert a little leadership, integrity and authority. 'Forget about giving us a share of this, Ronnie, you can have the lot. Broccoli pays us good money anyway and it's not worth the risk of us getting caught for a few grand. Just promise me that not a soul will know you're coming up to Belem with us, I don't want any trouble.'

'On my son's life, John. Nobody's going to know a thing. Only, when you get my air ticket to fly up to Belem and back, you'd better not book in my name. Make it in the name of Brown or Jones . . .,' he smirked, '. . . or Slipper.'

I roared with laughter. 'Airline tickets, Ronnie my boy. Who the fuck do you think you're dealing with, *Opportunity Knocks*? We are the James Bond crew! Airline tickets are for peasants. You're a celebrity and you've got to think like one. I'll fly you there on a private jet!'

It was settled. We would leave in a week's time. The yacht was already waiting at Belem. I could now brief the crew about my departure plans. I called Santos Dumont Airport and gave them plenty of advance warning about filing flight plans for the Lear jet. Then I phoned back to Britain and warned Gavin Goodwin to get ready to move to the Caribbean with a photographer.

Fred, Norrie and I had a good drink that night. It looked as if we were going to pull it off. At least there was no doubt the bait had been well and truly taken and the net was closing. Ronnie was just like one of those monkeys from my Rhodesian childhood. His fist was clenched so tightly that he didn't have the sense to let go. Except the net wasn't closing on Ronnie Biggs. We didn't know at the time, but it was closing on us!

I moved the team to the Hotel Gloria, not far from the airport, the night before we were due to fly out. All the luggage was transferred there, including the marquee valise which would have been used to transport Biggs if he got cold feet at the last moment. But I was confident the valise wouldn't be necessary. Biggs was co-operating fully, the yacht was on standby, we still had a contingency fund left in the budget, and our security had been watertight. Well, maybe watertight, but certainly not alcohol proof.

Fleet Street, the centre of the newspaper publishing business in Britain, runs on booze and gossip. The bigger the story, the more drinking and small talk. And, of course, they all hate each other. It's not just bitchiness between rivals. They would stitch up their own mates who work on the same paper in the hopes of getting their jobs. In the week between Biggs walking into my trap and his next appointment at the *delegacia*, he had begun to receive a series of phone calls. They were tip-offs from the *Daily Star* office in Manchester, warning Biggs that he was about to be kidnapped by three former Scots Guards who were 'ex-commandos and very dangerous!' There was even a phone call by a journalist from the New York office of the *Daily Mirror*, the newspaper group which wanted Gavin to write the exclusive. This call was to one of Biggs's girlfriends and the reporter said he thought Biggs had already been kidnapped and was on the high seas.

The inevitable happened. I turned up at the bar opposite the *delegacia*, ready to escort Ronnie back to the Hotel Gloria for a drink before we set off for the airport. I saw Ronnie arrive and go into the police station. A few minutes later he walked out on to the pavement and I stood up from my table outside the bar and began to walk across the street to meet him.

'That's him,' Ronnie screamed. And the doors of the *delegacia* burst open and a squad of Rio cops with guns poured out, stopped the traffic and hustled me off in a paddy wagon. I could see Ronnie grinning and waving as I was driven off. He was the Master of Escape. First, Wandsworth Prison, then Slipper, and now Miller. There was nobody who could touch him. On the outside I was calm and unruffled. Inside I was seething. Someone was going to pay for this.

Back at the hotel Fred and Norrie were captured and driven to join me at police headquarters. It was all a ghastly mistake, I was telling the Chief of Police. Biggs had been pestering me and my film crew for money, I explained. And there would be big trouble over this, I warned. The James Bond movie-makers were big spenders and the entire country of Brazil would be black-listed for all future movie production unless I was released immediately with my men. Cubby Broccoli would wreck their economy if they messed with us. There was also the little matter of a Lear jet waiting at Santos Dumont airport with the meter ticking over. That charter alone was costing 20,000 dollars and would probably be deducted from the Chief's salary. And there was the charter fee for my yacht in Belem.

That was enough. The Chief ordered his clerk, Luis Cobra, to take us back to our hotel, collect our luggage and get us started on our journey out of the country. We dragged our belongings from the Hotel Gloria and Luis Cobra began to grin widely when he saw the marquee valise. 'For carrying camera tripods and cans of film,' I explained.

'No,no, I theenk for carrying Señor Biggs,' he laughed. 'This is Brazil, Señor Miller. We know about these things.'

We sat glumly in the paddy wagon taking us to the airport and Cobra said cheerfully, 'You give my regards to your Superintendent Sleeper when you get back to Scot-land Yard. Oh, and by the way, you no try thees again, please.'

'I don't know who the hell or what the hell you're talking about,' I protested.

Cobra made a great display of being irritated and losing his patience. 'The only reason you and your officers are not arrested is we do not like to put policemen, not even British policemen, in our jails. Scotland Yard must be very desperate men to try thees. But now you try two times and you fail two times. Please do not try again. You cannot win.'

At the airport he saluted each of us in turn and gave us our passports back. And the pilot examined our passports, and he too saluted and began bowing and scraping.

On the flight to Belem, I couldn't come to terms with our bad luck – and our good luck. We all still travelled on the passports we used while in the Army. They were still valid for a couple of years. The standard ten-year British passport contains a page for a photo of the holder, together with physical description – and a definition of the holder's occupation. Members of the military are not described as 'soldier' or 'sailor' or 'airman'. That could cause raised eyebrows at Third World passport control desks. We all had an accurate, if misleading, passport classification: one bold line which said, Occupation: Government Service.

The Rio cops genuinely did think we were Scotland Yard, or at least that we worked for some shady branch of Her Majesty's Government.

We sailed back to Antigua in sullen silence and I vowed to myself I would go back and get Ronnie Biggs. I had tried with gentle persuasion and I had trusted a journalist to keep a secret. It hadn't worked. It was the most crippling sense of failure I'd experienced since I'd tried it on with a young lady in the back of an armoured personnel carrier at the Guards' depot back in 1963. She had slapped my face. That had been humiliating, especially as she had a terrific little figure but at least I hadn't spent a fortune on her, 3s. 6d. if I remember right. I'd bought her a couple of lager and limes. This time I'd spent £50,000. Not my own money of course, but it was still quite a lot of money if you had nothing to show for it at the end.

I don't like failure. I don't like being made to look stupid. I'd failed with Ronnie Biggs and I'd looked stupid. The more I thought about it, the more I wanted to get even. I mean, yes, I had other ambitions. I liked putting on the style. I liked money and the things money can buy.

Champagne; Rolls-Royces; beautiful women. But you could keep all those if I could take Biggs out of Brazil. He had now become an obsession. I had to go back and get him. I needed to get even. I thought of the noble and honourable motto of the Scots Guards – *Nemo Me Impune Lacessit*. That's Latin. It means 'Nobody messes with me and gets away with it.' I thought of the simple motto of Executive Security: Get the Bastards! Next time I wasn't going to be Mister Nice Guy.

Biggs Two

There was no way I could get funding from the same source again. And no way I could face Stephen Bentinck. I gave up the security contract with him and the rent-free office. There were no recriminations about having blown his money. I had to eat some shit, but not a lot. I blamed myself. The one fatal flaw in my plan had been the handling of the media. I'd have my revenge on them sooner or later. In the meantime I went back to showbusiness security work, tour managing for rock 'n' roll bands and even dabbling again in running music clubs.

My abortive attempt to snatch Biggs had made some headlines but it had all seemed like such a half-arsed amateur stunt that the ripple of publicity soon died down. Still, I couldn't go for a quiet drink in most of the West End clubs or my old Army haunts without someone making a joke at my expense. I had been cultivating some high flying security work among upper-echelon government contacts and important political movers and shakers, and now I was getting paranoid about my credibility being in tatters. I was obsessed with getting back to Brazil and capturing Biggs for real.

The Biggs Affair had brought me some publicity, but not the kind I wanted. Some top-level people thought it showed I had style, and I was offered a few overseas contracts, but always as number two on a big operation. I didn't want that. Other people who sniffed a quick buck,

135

told me I could have made a fortune from Fleet Street if I had pulled off the Biggs snatch. I was quite prepared to let them harp on about the missed opportunity for making cash.

It took eighteen months before I was ready to move again. There were people with money to invest who were willing to back me with cash to fund another run to Rio. All they wanted was the exclusive rights to sell the story when I got a successful result. They were welcome to that. But I wasn't dealing with a bored rich kid like Stephen Bentinck this time. I was in the hands of men who saw the financing of a Ronnie Biggs snatch as a profitable investment. To earn any respect from them, and to make sure I kept total operational control, I had to match the money they were prepared to put up. And I was stony broke.

I turned to Sir Hugh Fraser, Baronet. Hugh had approached me sympathetically after the abortive Biggs attempt. 'You win some and you lose some, John,' Sir Hugh had told me. He offered me some very lucrative work – how can I say? – sorting out some problems surrounding Harrods. I turned him down. Sir Hugh persisted. He lectured me about learning from experience, water under the bridge, fresh challenges . . . he was trying to snap me out of my fit of depression. Sir Hugh was a friend and I wanted to help him. But first I had to rid myself of the recurring nightmare of Ronnie Biggs grinning at me. I had a couple of new partners for another attempt, one, a businessman who published medical and pharmaceutical trade magazines and Pat King, an ex-café owner with a thriving minicab business who wanted to be an active participant. That's when I fixed up the meeting with Sir Hugh at the penthouse in Barker's department store in Kensington High Street and he agreed to pick up my share of the tab in exchange for my undivided attention in the future.

It wouldn't need to be quite so expensive. I'd done the

recce already. In fact I'd done a complete dry run. I could go straight in this time. Just fly to Antigua and charter a boat. Sail down to Belem, pick up Biggs in Rio, sail back. We'd skip the Presidential suite in the Copacabana Palace this time around. Make it an economy-class operation.

The first problem with another snatch operation was finding a boat. That was easy first time round but might be more of a problem this time. There were only about fifteen charter skippers on Antigua and they all talked. The minute some tall, determined-looking Brit started muttering about taking a boat down to Belem, the first thing they would remember would be what had happened less than a couple of years before. They'd be bound to twig that we were making a second attempt on Biggs.

Still, Antigua remained the best place and all we could do was try. So Pat King, my new partner, flew out with me to try to fix the right vessel. The funny thing was that almost the first person we bumped into was Steve Adamson, skipper of the yacht I'd used last time around. Pat and I were just walking into the bar of the Admiral's Inn in English Harbour and who should be there at the counter but Adamson. I turned right round and went back to my hotel room. Pat was pretty confused. I explained who Adamson was and asked Pat to get him up to my room. If Adamson knew why we were there, we might as well pack up and go home. I had to sort him out. Pat's a pretty smooth talker and he persuaded Adamson to come upstairs. I'll always remember it. The door opened and all Adamson saw was me standing there with a drink in my hand, grinning. He really did look as if he'd seen a ghost. He had a drink in his hand too. He dropped his.

I did a perfectly straightforward number on him. I just told him a lot of people had a serious financial stake in this operation and that it wouldn't do for word to get out about what we were planning. In particular, I said, if word got out through him, then my friends might be sufficiently agitated to want to execute some form of reprisal. Well, that certainly made *him* agitated. I think he had visions of a kneecapping, IRA-style. He was out of my room before you could say 'kidnap'. Wouldn't even accept another drink. He just couldn't wait to scarper. We watched him pull up his anchor and leave harbour right there and then. The poor man couldn't even hang around until morning.

Pat turned in early that night. The experience had left him very subdued and I think he could see our joint funds vanishing into the balmy Antiguan air. I had other ideas. I have never been one for early nights and I've always believed in creating my own luck. So I thought I'd go for a late night stroll. Inevitably I found that after a while I was nearing the local disco. It was a two-storey floating nightclub, connected to the beach by a 30-foot gang-plank and secured by a single rope knotted round a palm tree. Very Caribbean! As I was setting foot on the gang-plank I heard raised voices, one of them Scottish. It was a familiar scene: an angry, not quite sober Scot being kicked out of a nightclub by a couple of bouncers. When I gently inquired if I might help sort out the problem, the two bouncers decided they'd got a Scottish invasion on their hands and told me my presence was definitely not welcome.

Back on the beach we introduced ourselves. My fellow countryman turned out to be a genial guy named Thorfin McIvor. He apologised for having got me turned off the floating disco before I'd even boarded it. 'Not to worry,' I assured him, 'I should think it's full of loose women, strong drink and loud music. Not my scene at all.' My next request took him by surprise. 'Do you have a knife?'

Thorfin said that, irritated though he was at being bounced off the disco, there was no need to go stabbing anyone on his behalf. I reassured him and rather reluctantly he handed over one of the most sophisticated Swiss

138

Army knives. His face was a picture as I sawed through the rope which moored the disco to the palm tree. As the whole edifice started to drift out to sea to the beat of the Bee Gees and a buzz of girlish laughter, he put a hand on my shoulder and said, one grateful Scot to another, 'Can I buy you a drink?'

Thorfin was a find. He hailed from Hawick in the Scottish borders and he was a solid six-foot first-class rugby player. Very much my sort of man. He was also the skipper of a yacht, the *Now Can I Too*, a 70-foot boat owned by a Texan millionaire, Bob Sebinski. I explained that Pat and I were working for Project 90, a film and video unit which just happened to have some extremely smart headed notepaper. The film company spoof had worked so well the first time round that I had decided to use the same cover to explain why we carried so much camera gear, extremely large canvas bags and threw money around in great quantities of ready cash. We were plotting an underwater shoot by an oil rig in the Amazon Basin and needed a yacht just like the *Now Can I Too*.

Next morning Pat and I were introduced to Thorfin's boss over coffee on board ship. Within minutes we had shaken hands on a deal. Thorfin was to be ready to sail for our old stamping ground, the port of Belem, in two weeks' time. I promised that when we returned I would bring a load of charts of the area from London. The *Now Can I Too* was a beautiful boat: all teak finish on a fibreglass hull. We'd swung from the disaster of a chance meeting with Steve Adamson to the triumph of a chance meeting with Thorfin McIvor. So you see what I mean about creating your own luck!

I'd already recruited my team. Fred again. Fred always worked for me even if it was just bouncing drunks out of pubs. But as for Norrie, no. I'm afraid Norrie had been badly rattled last time round when we had been captured. I didn't even want to offer him the choice of a place on this trip. I knew he would have refused and that might have left me with a security leak at home. I took Tony Marriage, an SAS-trained trooper I'd worked with in the past. He was just recovering from a bad bout of hepatitis he'd contracted in the Middle East. I thought a spell in the Caribbean might help him to recuperate. And I enlisted Mark Aldgate who had done some club and security work for me. Mark was fit and full of initiative and I knew him and trusted him.

We all flew out together via New York with about forty grand stuffed into money belts. It's a strange experience getting drunk in Times Square with a fortune round your waist! Then in Antigua we met up with Thorfin who had used the up-front money from the charter fee to install a sophisticated satellite navigation system in the boat. With those electronics and my new charts we had every chance of not getting lost.

Thorfin's crew consisted of a mate from North Carolina, Greg Nelson, and Veronica Pettito, a stunning Scottish-Italian girl with raven hair and terrific tits who did the cooking.

First of all we sailed south east to Barbados where we dropped off Pat and Tony. They back-tracked, flying to Miami and then direct to Rio. They were our advance party. Their strength was that neither of them knew Biggs and he didn't know them. Pat didn't look like a solider on a clandestine mission. He looked like what he was, the owner of a cab business. He would pose as a freelance magazine photographer and offer Biggs money to act as a guide in Rio and to pose for a few photos. I knew Ronnie's natural greed would do the rest. Tony was well trained in SAS sneaky surveillance techniques. He would tail both of them without being seen. I wanted to make sure that Pat had some back-up if Ronnie or any of his neighbours or police smelt a rat.

Our journey to Belem took us about ten days which gave

140

us an opportunity to get to know the crew better. I found I
felt sick if I spent too much time below, so I spent most of
the day on the deck and slept there at night, tied in a
canvas sail bag. One night, under the tropical stars off the
coast of South America, Thorfin and I were alone when he
suddenly said, 'John, if you don't tell me what's really
going on I'm turning the boat around and going home.'

Not to put too fine a point on it Thorfin had figured out
we weren't who we claimed to be. He had watched us
going through our paces with all this hi-tech film equipment we had picked up from a rental company in Soho
before we left London. We had tried to pass Fred off as an
expert sound recordist. It was as classic a piece of mis-
casting as asking Arnold Schwarzenegger to play Albert
Schweitzer. Every time Fred went near the audio tape
equipment he'd ram a microphone lead into the wrong
socket or spool the tape reels backwards or break something off. Fred's fine at handling general purpose
machine-guns with belts of full metal jackets, but give
him anything less robust than forged steel and it's like
putting a butterfly in a blender. Besides, there aren't
that many documentary film crews who all have their
blood groups tattooed on their left arms.

Thorfin was a bright guy. He knew by the way we talked
among ourselves that we were all army or ex-army. I had
been half prepared for this and I remembered how effective the 'Government Service' passport entry had been in
our brush with the Brazilian authorities the last time
around. 'Thorfin,' I said, 'I'd love to tell you what's going
on but it's a hush-hush operation and I simply don't have
the authority.' Thorfin only half bought this, so I said, 'I
tell you what. If you let me use the radio I'll file a request
for clearance so I can brief you on our mission.' He agreed
to this and I sent off a nonsense message to a pre-arranged
contact. He sent an equally silly reply which I went
through the elaborate charade of decoding. Then I let

Thorfin in on our little secret. The only white lie I told him was that we were on Her Majesty's Secret Service. He thought about it and said, 'Count me in.' From that moment on he was one of the team.

The rest of the journey down was uneventful but we almost blew it in Belem. Brazilians are terrible crooks and they were always trying it on. For instance, I always ask a taxi driver how much I owe them, even if it's clearly displayed on the meter. It's fair to assume there's gonna be some hidden surcharge, so I ask. Every time I asked in Brazil, they'd multiply it by five. So I was always having these rows with taxi drivers there.

We'd arrived in Belem at dusk and went ashore for a drinking party without any passport or customs checks. About midnight, coming back, we had to get a ferry – just a rickety little punt – out to the *Now Can I Too*. Before we got in, I asked how much it would be. The boatman said a hundred cruzeiros each. Fair enough. But as we got nearer our ritzy glitzy yacht you could feel him saying to himself, 'Hey, *hombre*, these aren't just drunken oil rig hooligans I've got here, these are rich guys.' So when we came to pay, he suddenly said, '*Five* hundred cruzeiros each.' I wasn't having that, so I gave him a five-hundred note for all of us. He didn't like that and he stood there in his little punt carrying on in Portuguese like an old fishwife. Fred and I threw a couple of boathooks at him. They went straight through the bottom of his boat and he started sinking, whereupon the Harbour Police came out. We were all fighting drunk, there was a terrible scene and we were lucky not to be arrested.

Next morning my blood ran cold just thinking about it. We had arrived at dusk because we knew Customs worked Brazilian office hours, which are approximately 11 a.m. to lunch. I wanted myself and the team off the boat before they got to us so we left the ship's boy and our one woman on board to cope with Customs and got the first flight to Rio. At the airport Tony met us and said, 'Bad news, guys.'

It turned out that Biggs had moved from his old suburban house at Sepetiba into a high-rise building on Botafogo Beach, not far from Santos Dumont Airport. It was good news that it was so close to the airport but it was an apartment block with heavy security. Guards, close-circuit TV, German shepherds, the whole caboodle. I wasn't too happy with that, but Pat King had spun his yarn to Biggs about photographic assignments, Ronnie had swallowed it and they were getting along just fine. There were six of my team in Rio now, and we were itching to go. Pat had arranged a meeting with Ronnie that evening in a local restaurant.

We immediately hit the local Hertz office and rented an eight-seat VW minibus, drove it into an alleyway a few streets away, ripped out the seats, and distributed them to the local kids as German designer furniture for their living rooms. Then I drilled some holes in the sides of the VW for us to spy through. We were all going to be lying on the floor immediately prior to the snatch. Tony Marriage's sense of decency and responsibility caused him to complain that we were ruining his Hertz credit rating with all this vandalism!

On the floor of the minibus was a marquee valise, just like the one we had 'borrowed' from the Quartermaster's stores at the Guards' depot the first time around. I had also cut off strips of white surgical adhesive tape, about forty in all, to fix all the essential gags and bindings on Ronnie. We had circular pads for his eyes and wax for his ears. Total sensory deprivation was what we were after. He'd be less of a problem that way. He wouldn't know which way up he was. There was ice in the bag to keep him nice and cool. We could have used some of that ice ourselves because it was 105 degrees. And we carried some lengths of hosepipe with lead weights. No knives. No guns.

Everything went according to schedule at first. Pat showed up in a cab, went into the restaurant and ordered a drink. We waited. And we waited. Three God-awful hours in that sweltering heat. Ronnie didn't show. Pat started to panic. He came out of the restaurant and made as if to come over to the V W to talk to us. Thorfin slid out of the driver's seat and headed him off. He got alongside and whispered out of the corner of his mouth, 'Get back in there, Pat!' That made Pat even more jittery. It was frustrating as hell for me, but I dared not show my face in case Ronnie came round the corner and spotted me. Eventually I had to abort. It was an expensive setback. The Lear jet was already on standby at the airport to take us to Belem. Ten thousand dollars gone. The budget was horribly tight.

The following day a very nervous Pat King phoned Ronnie and then relayed the message to me. Ronnie hadn't got suspicious, he'd got drunk. He'd fallen asleep and missed the meeting. But he sensed he had Pat on some kind of hook so he took advantage, typically, and suggested a meeting that night at an expensive restaurant at Sugar Loaf mountain. Pat agreed, but his nerves were getting the better of him. He was convinced we were walking into a trap. He was excused duties from then on. I told him he could grab a plane out of Rio for Miami that day so he wouldn't even be in the country when the snatch took place.

Now I was getting desperate. We'd just have to go to Ronnie's flat and snatch him there. Too bad about the security. But when we got there next night, we saw two cops outside smoking cigarettes. Real cops. Not deadbeat goons hired by the local residents' association. These were real policemen with guns. No way could we get past them, let alone come back out dragging Ronnie. Never mind.

Now to contingency plan B. We'd wait at the end of the street and grab him out of sight of the security cops. But dammit, as soon as he left his front door a cab pulled up and he got in. The only answer was plan C. We knew where he was going and we'd grab him between the cab and the restaurant at the other end. Thorfin gunned the VW and we drove so fast to Sugar Loaf that we were there ahead of Ronnie. The second his cab pulled up we piled out of the van and started to close in on him. The only trouble was that a luxury coach arrived at the same moment and about sixty American tourists disembarked and began milling around the entrance to the restaurant. So all these guys were elbowing their way through the crowd to get at Ronnie and I was shouting, 'No, no, you're crazy, get back in the van!' Pandemonium!

Eventually I got everyone back in the van without Ronnie seeing us and when we peered out through our observation holes we saw that Ronnie had gone into the open air bar and was sitting at a table having a beer. He was surrounded by about three hundred people, and he was innocently looked around to see if Pat King was there. We had no plans left. This was a desperate situation and it called for desperate measures. I told Tony and Mark to get as close as possible to him, using a low wall as cover. We drove the van right up to the wall. They were to go in, grab him, shout, 'Right', as soon as they'd done the deed. Then I would spring from the van and join in.

Off they raced. I crouched out of sight in the back of the van and I heard tables falling over. Then the cry of 'Right!' and I was out, over the wall and taking the stairs three at a time. Ronnie was struggling. Tony had him by the neck. Mark had his hands. I grabbed him around the waist. 'What the fuck's going on? Let me go! Help! Help!' Ronnie was shouting blue murder and kicking out like a young donkey. Down the stairs we went with him grabbing everything in sight – tables, chairs, waiters, customers.

No one got to their feet. The three hundred customers just looked on, fascinated. They must have thought it was part of the cabaret. He put up quite a fight but it took us only ten seconds to get him down to the van. As we got him to the vehicle, he got his hands free and tried holding on to the sides of the door but I kicked his fingertips and socked him in the jaw. We bundled him inside.

Meanwhile, Rio de Janeiro's oldest popcorn seller had parked his cart right in front of our VW. Maybe he thought he could do some trade among the crowd who were slowly beginning to gather. Fred, in his own friendly way, asked him to move on, but the old boy objected. So Fred just lifted him and his cart and threw both of them aside. It was chaos! Thorfin pulled away smartish, careful not to gun the engine into causing wheelspin. We didn't want to attract more attention with screeching tyres like a gangster B-movie. It was worse. It sounded like a rattle of small arms fire as we slithered away across a sea of popcorn.

We had Ronnie stuffed into the bag within seconds, lying on his back on a bed of ice cubes, staring up through the zip opening. I was ready now for my triumphal address to the Great Train Robber. 'I have returned ... He who laughs last ... Justice has triumphed ...' I needed to break the strained muffled silence with a memorable epithet which would rank alongside 'The eagle has landed' or 'Never in the field of human conflict ...' Fred beat me to it. He shoved his big face into the valise with a beaming smile and roared: 'Never expected to see me again did you, you old bastard?' I never said a word. Maybe I would have been tempting fate if I had.

I needed Ronnie to give up the struggle pretty quickly, so I leaned over and showed him I had a hypodermic needle in one hand and a lead cosh in the other. 'You can have the sodium pentathol or a whack across the head,' I told him. He was shaking his head furiously.

'Wanna come quietly?' I asked.

Ronnie nodded in agreement. My worst moment had passed. I could never have hit him once we had him in virtual captivity. And the hypodermic was filled with nothing more mind-bending than tap water. 'OK, Ronnie,' I said. 'We're going away some distance for a quiet talk with you. Just stay still and don't attract any attention to us if you know what's good for you.' He agreed. I put the pads over his eyes and wax plugs in his ears and zipped up the valise.

We'd calculated four-and-a-half minutes to Santos Dumont Airport. Our only moment of apprehension was when we heard the wail of a police siren right behind us. The contingency plan if we were caught was to roll Ronnie right out of the back of the VW and keep moving. Then if we were stopped we'd say we'd just been horsing around. Didn't kidnap anyone, officer, honest. Scout's honour. We'd say we'd just dragged Ronnie out of the bar as a practical joke. The police car sailed past without giving us a second look.

I was dripping with sweat when we reached Santos Dumont. It was searingly hot and I had been working hard. Now I had to go into the airport building and wander into the Lear charter office looking cool and nonchalant. It was fairly essential to blend in, because of course all the staff *were* cool and nonchalant. The girl gave me a soft drink and checked the documents. The captain came through in his uniform and wished me good evening and asked if I wanted to leave now. I said yes and although he didn't actually say '*mañana*' that was obviously what he had in mind because he sat down with a coffee and started chatting up the girl.

I stepped up to him and asked briskly, 'All right if I bring my film crew through the office?'

'Sure, sir.'

'And just one piece of equipment?'

'No problem, how heavy's the equipment?'

'Oh, I'd say about a hundred and sixty pounds. And I want it to travel in the passenger compartment with me.'

The captain shrugged. 'I'll just mark it down as another body. Call it six passengers instead of five, for the load-master's benefit.'

We were using a Lear 25. It could handle the weight and the range.

'That's fine,' I agreed. 'You won't be far wrong. I'll tell them to come along now.'

'No hurry,' he said.

I ducked into the parking lot. 'OK guys,' I said. 'We're going to walk out of here and over to the plane and we're going to act natural. Chat, whistle, hum, stay together. We go straight past all these crowds in the lounge; straight through the office; out on to the tarmac.' It was an internal flight so there were no Customs or passport controls.

People do tend to stare at four guys carrying a dirty great canvas bag with four handles on it. It's bound to look as if they're carrying a corpse. No disguising it. I walked on ahead, whistling a happy tune and the others chatted among themselves. I was afraid Ronnie's ice was going to start melting. I didn't want him to drown. I could only imagine what he must have been thinking inside the valise. If we hadn't stuffed his ears he would have clearly heard the echoing of airport departure lounge announcements and then the whine of jet engines on the tarmac.

He must have heard some of it. We manhandled the bag on to the back seat of the Lear and we all took our seats. Then just as the co-pilot was checking our seat belts, I noticed the bag was moving and wriggling. And the co-pilot noticed it. And the co-pilot saw that I saw. He looked at me and I looked at him. Then he looked away and he went back to the pilot and he said something in Portuguese. It sounded bad. I don't know the Portuguese for,

148

'Hey, that fucking bag's moving,' but I've a hunch that's what he said. So I took a few paces up the aisle to the flight deck and said to the pilot in English, 'You're probably wondering about the bag moving around.'

'Now you say so, señor, I am, how you say, curious.'

'It's OK,' I assured him. 'We're a wildlife film crew. We've got an anaconda snake in the bag. We borrowed him from a zoo in Belem and he's going home. We fed him a couple of chickens on the way to the airport and he's just sort of stretching his legs after dinner. He won't cause any bother.'

The pilot turned to his co-pilot and began to mutter. His number two had already heard the word 'anaconda' and his eyebrows had vanished up behind his cap badge. They shrugged and taxied out for take-off.

Ronnie might not have seen or heard a thing, but he couldn't have helped noticing the high speed vibration, the sudden tilt of about thirty degrees and the feeling in the pit of the stomach as the Lear rocketed off the runway. He was frantically trying to wriggle out of his bindings. I had to open the bag and threaten him again with the needle. His eyes were still covered and I held the hypodermic along the side of his cheek so he could feel the sharp outline. He settled down again with a soft, muffled groan.

Fred had already broached the in-flight fridge and was passing round the shrimps and chilled champagne. 'We've done it, we've done it,' he was chortling.

'No, we haven't,' I said. 'At least not yet.' And for the rest of the flight you could feel us all wanting to shout out we'd done it but knowing that we couldn't and shouldn't.

The ice in Ronnie's valise was starting to melt and I didn't want him getting pneumonia, so we persuaded the pilot to turn up the cabin heat to over a hundred degrees. By now the pilot thought we were a very strange bunch – he couldn't wait to get rid of us.

It took about three hours to reach Belem. We got there about 2 a.m. and as we circled to land I was watching for a line of flashing blue lights that would signal a waiting police committee. Nothing. Ronnie had told his neighbours in Rio that he was going out drinking again, so his absence still hadn't been noticed. And nobody at the Sugar Loaf restaurant had thought our snatch anything more than an elaborate motorised mugging.

The pilot parked a long way away from the terminal and we said goodnight politely and lugged the valise over to where we'd left our hire car. It had gone. God knows where – you can't trust anyone these days! We ended up taking a taxi down to the harbour. When we got there it was all locked up and we had to dodge the guard *and* get ourselves and Ronnie over a ten-foot fence. God bless the training and experience of army assault courses, is all I can say. It was a good thing we didn't drop him.

At the quayside we flashed a signal out to the yacht, which was moored about 150 yards out in midstream. Greg came across in the Zodiac and ferried us out. He didn't know about Ronnie. I'd told him we'd gone to Rio to pick up some underwater filming equipment. So he wasn't too surprised to see the valise. But he did get a shock when I ripped it open in mid-stream and he saw this grey-haired bloke with blood all over his face who sat up and started mumbling through his gag. Poor old Ronnie! He was in a terrible state, but he was alive. Within minutes he'd be under sail, by daylight he would be in international waters.

Once I'd made sure everything was under control, I lit out. I knew I'd be the prime suspect as soon as Ronnie's disappearance had been reported and someone tied it in with the abduction at the Sugar Loaf restaurant. I had to be elsewhere to set up a smoke screen. A few hours later I was back at Belem Airport. From there I flew to Caracas in Venezuela and on to Miami where I was first to give Pat King the good news. Biggs was in the bag!

Within twenty-four hours the word was out in Fleet Street that Ronnie Biggs had gone off for a rendezvous with a photographer and was missing. I made sure I was keeping a high profile in Florida. The serialisation of Ronnie's own book had just coincidentally begun in Rupert Murdoch's *Sun* newspaper and when curious newsmen phoned me in the US, I told them I thought the crafty old rascal was up to some PR hype to boost sales. I never realised that serious panic was setting in with Ronnie's publishers in London. If he had been kidnapped and ended up in a British court facing jailbreak charges, the book would have to be withdrawn from the shelves to avoid prejudicing any new court proceedings.

Pat King and his trade magazine contact in London were also having some problems. They were sounding out the prospects of selling the exclusive story for £100,000. But those Fleet Street newspapers who didn't believe Ronnie's disappearance was a publishing hype were determined to expose his abductors. And the papers were full of dire warnings from the London underworld of what terrible revenge would be taken on Ronnie's kidnappers. Pat and the magazine publisher were having second thoughts on whether publicising themselves by offering the sale of the story was going to be worth coping with the threats from Ronnie's fellow crooks. Me? I was in my element.

After a few days it was time to leave Florida and move back into the Caribbean. The first reason was to get married. I wasn't quite ready to show my hand to Fleet Street yet and my fiancée, Sarah, had joined me in Florida. We had planned for some time to get married and this seemed the ideal opportunity. I think Sarah may have had second thoughts about a wedding while this whole Biggs circus was getting under way but, good girl that she is, she ended up agreeing wholeheartedly.

Sarah and I had met some time before when I was running a club for Richard Branson called the Venue, near Victoria Station in London. She had arrived in the company of a guy who knew one of the club staff and they joined us in my private manager's bar upstairs, reserved for VIPs and selected guests. I fell for her immediately and I'd discreetly wheedled out of her the fact that she worked as a supervisor at the department store, Dickins and Jones. The following day I'd paid a visit to her on the third floor of the store, much to her embarrassment, and later when she finished work that day, I whisked her away for a drink in the Cinderella Bar and a cosy theatre box laid on for me by my friend John Avery who was the manager at the London Palladium. I was being at my charming best but I was still locked in the tail end of a relationship with a girl who shared a flat with me.

There was nothing for it. I moved out, away from my girlfriend, and took a mews flat of my own in Kensington while I wooed Sarah. A few weeks later she graciously moved in with me to the great astonishment and, I think, displeasure of her parents, especially her father who is an ex-Cavalry officer and merchant banker who viewed me with some suspicion. I think they have both probably warmed to me a wee bit since the births of their two lovely grand-children. But at that time Sarah didn't know much about the planning of the Biggs snatch and as we had both set our hearts on a Caribbean wedding anyway, at least I had some explanation for my presence there if, and when, the press first caught up with me.

If everything went according to plan, Ronnie was to be landed in Antigua and the *Now Can I Too* would have to sail past Barbados to reach the island. I planned to get married and then intercept the yacht and sail the last leg to Antigua with my captive. A bit of style and swank, I thought. A massive 'I told you so' to Stephen Bentinck and a sly, secret wink to the TV cameras for Sir Hugh Fraser.

It was when I hit Barbados that all hell was let loose. There had been an English Test cricket tour of the West Indies and a fiasco in Guyana where my old friend Forbes Burnham had objected to the English team because one of their players had taken part in a game in South Africa. They weren't so fussy in Barbados, so the cricketers had rearranged their itinerary to take in an extra match. It all boiled down to one thing; the British press and television were in Barbados in some strength by the time I got there. From the moment I arrived I was plastered all over the front pages and the TV screens. Biggs was still on the high seas and the Brazilians were screaming at the British ambassador in Brasilia, the Foreign Office and Scotland Yard with equal measures of hysteria.

They had even sent Brazilian Air Force planes out over the Atlantic to make low passes over the *Now Can I Too* but all they had returned with were baffling telephotos of a grey-haired man with a broken nose and beer gut giving them unmistakeably obscene gestures with his fingers. That was Freddie Prime. Biggs was always kept below whenever planes appeared on the horizon.

Below decks Ronnie had managed to wreak some damage. Still within a couple of hundred miles of the Brazilian coast he had been successful in jamming the engine pumps in the hope of flooding the yacht and forcing Thorfin to turn back towards Belem. He had tried to bribe Fred and the others once my back was turned: he lied that he had a fortune from the proceeds of the Great Train Robbery still tucked away, and it could all be theirs. When that failed, he revealed to Fred the true identities of the two men he said were the masterminds behind the robbery who had never been caught.

One of the names was that of a very senior and highly regarded British Army officer, who now lives a life of some luxury in retirement. Maybe there was some 'military precision' in the Robbery after all. This famous military man could not afford to have Biggs back in a courtroom, possibly revealing his secrets in exchange for sympathy from the judge. He'd mount an operation to kill them all if it looked as though the Train Robber was to be deported back to Britain, Ronnie warned. Fred was impressed but he still wouldn't give in to temptation.

Once in Barbados, at least I was in radio contact with the yacht. I arranged to rendezvous with them on the high seas, six miles off Barbados in international waters, under cover of darkness, to board the yacht and personally take charge of Biggs. There was just the matter of my wedding to take care of.

The ceremony was at the Holiday Inn in Bridgetown and it was attended by the entire press corps. An agitated Pat King was there with his wife, coming under increasing pressure from the financial backers in London to cut and run and to hell with the money. Jim Davidson, the comedian, and a good friend, was a witness and provided an impromptu cabaret performance at our little reception.

I was called away to receive a discreet call of congratulation from Sir Hugh Fraser. No, he wasn't calling from Harrods, he told me. And not from Barker's department store in Kensington, or from his Scottish newspaper offices in Glasgow. He was less than a mile away, at the Sandy Lane hotel in Barbados. He was there with his girlfriend Annabel Findlay. The chairman of Harrods couldn't resist flying out to be there, getting a grandstand view of how his money was being spent.

I tried vainly to make sure the pressmen got more champagne than they could handle. After the wedding reception I planned to sneak away to a lonely spot outside Bridgetown, where I had hidden a Zodiac with a 40-h.p. Johnson outboard, and then sail off to board the yacht. Darkness was falling when I got the disastrous radio message. Thorfin had sailed as close to Barbados as he dared to make the rendezvous. The engine was out of action on the yacht because of Ronnie's sabotage. Under Thorfin's expert helmsmanship with generous cruising sails, the yacht was in no danger. But without the engine, he was at the mercy of the wind and tide when it came to fine manoeuvring. He had drifted in just a little too close – and he had been captured by the one and only Barbadian gunboat.

I sent another round of champagne to the press corps and drifted slowly up to my bedroom with my new bride, aware of the close scrutiny and knowing winks of the Fleet Street hacks. Then I jumped out of the window of the bridal suite and made off into the darkness.

Waiting for me down on the beach was a freelance journalist who had arrived on the island a few days before. Gerry Brown wasn't working with the pack. He had known from the moment the news broke that this was a real snatch. He was a contact of Fred Prime and he knew when Fred vanished from his regular haunts in London that something big was happening. Gerry didn't offer to buy any exclusive rights to the story. He just promised me he'd keep the rest of Fleet Street off my back. And he wanted to be the only journalist on board the yacht with Ronnie Biggs. I said, 'OK, you've got it.'

It took us about an hour to reach the yacht out on the ocean swell on a pitch black moonless night. It was a sorry sight. There was a tow rope from Barbados Coast Guard Vessel 501, the *George Fergusson*, firmly attached to the bow of the *Now Can I Too*.

We approached from the gunboat's blind side. Thorfin was on deck with hands cupped shouting across at me for instructions. Then the floodlights from the Coast Guard boat caught us fair and square. And a voice from a loudhailer boomed out, 'This vessel is under arrest, pull clear away!' There was the ripping sound of a canvas cover being pulled off a deck gun, so I throttled down and slipped into the pool of darkness in the wake of the yacht.

'Get Biggs on deck and throw him over to us,' I yelled, and Fred produced Ronnie on the heaving deck. Ronnie was gripping the deck rail, refusing to go over the side, Gerry Brown was threatening to leap the gap between our ships to board the yacht. And the Coast Guard were preparing to open fire. It was no good, I pulled back a hundred yards. Then I spotted them on the horizon – a flotilla of high speed launches closing in on us. It was Fleet Street on the high seas. They had hired everything in Bridgetown that floated and their convoy was bearing down on the gunboat and the yacht.

I pulled alongside the yacht once more and screamed at Tony Marriage, 'Get all the rolls of film and stills. Cut open a fender, stuff the film inside and throw it over to me.' It took a few minutes and by the time the white plastic fender had been launched into mid-air, a press launch was alongside and the blinding pops of flashguns were going off everywhere. The first flash caught the fender in mid-flight. And it looked for all the world like the sort of container that holds twenty kilos of cocaine. That was it. The Coast Guard thought the whole thing was a cover for a massive drugs run. The press pack saw Gerry ducking down on to the deck of our boat and in their panic they thought he was the Train Robber and Biggs had been transferred to our launch.

The gunboat turned a tight circle to catch us and seize our 'dope' and the *Now Can I Too* heeled over sharply as it was whipped round suddenly on the end of the tow rope. It was a carnival. I set off back towards the lights of Bridgetown with the press convoy in hot pursuit and the Coast Guard vanishing in our wake. Gerry and I landed on a deserted beach. The Fleet Street convoy cut their engines and hesitated. And then they steamed off again into the darkness back towards the Coast Guard and the yacht.

Two hours later Ronnie Biggs was landed at Bridgetown harbour where he felt the cold grasp of police handcuffs again for the first time since Slipper of the Yard had snapped bracelets on him five years before. Gerry secreted a dozen rolls of film in his bedroom and the Barbadian Special Branch came and arrested me and my new bride. Then they let us go. Then they arrested us again. And they let us go again. The crew of the yacht were slung into jail, in the cells next to Ronnie Biggs. Scotland Yard, red-faced and ranting, arrived in Barbados and began half-hearted extradition proceedings against Ronnie.

In London, the Friends of Ronnie Biggs had fund-raising parties in East End pubs to buy him the best international lawyers on the market and to threaten to track down the people who had masterminded his kidnap. Sir Hugh Fraser cut short his private holiday and slipped quietly back to his offices at Harrods, stifling a nervous laugh.

Sarah and I stayed in Barbados until I was assured that Thorfin and Fred and the rest of the crew of the *Now Can I Too* were released from Bridgetown jail and cleared to sail the yacht back to Antigua. We were followed several nights running by two plain clothes Barbadian policemen operating from the island's only unmarked police car – the most conspicuous white limo you've ever seen. Our room was searched several times so incompetently that if we'd had the entire team of Train Robbers zipped up there in canvas bags, they wouldn't have found them. It ended with me giving the Barbados Police Force informal extra tuition in search and surveillance techniques. They were surprisingly grateful.

I had some measure of revenge on the press. They

hounded me mercilessly. So I gave them merciless interviews. I told one Canadian reporter that my old granny had died in Motherwell, a penniless pensioner. I had promised her on her deathbed that I would capture Ronnie Biggs because when he robbed the train in 1963 he had stolen a mailbag which had held her winning football pools coupon and she had lost out on hundreds of thousands of pounds. The Brazilian TV programme, *Il Globo*, wouldn't swallow any explanations about justice and honour in my campaign to bring Biggs back before a British court. So I patiently explained to them that I'd done the whole thing to create a diplomatic incident between Britain and Brazil so that Brazil would break off relations with us and withdraw from the Soccer World Cup – giving Scotland an easy run to the final. Their reporter saw the blinding logic of it all and was delighted with his world scoop.

It was only a matter of time before Our Man from the High Commission turned up at my hotel, in a crumpled white cotton suit and mopping his brow with a handkerchief. 'Mr Miller,' he huffed and puffed. 'Her Majesty's Government would strenuously advise you to leave Barbados.'

I was moved. 'Tell Her Majesty I am deeply touched by her concern for me, but for her sake I am going to stay and see this through until that villain Biggs is brought to book for defying Her Majesty's law and sovereign authority.'

The man from the High Commission began to use distinctly undiplomatic language. 'Mr Miller, representatives of the Brazilian government are arriving on tomorrow's flight. They want Biggs returned to them. Oh – and they want you returned with him.'

'Why the hell do they want me?'

'They have a request for your extradition on a charge of kidnapping, Mr Miller.'

I thought about it. 'But they can't extradite me from a

former British colony to Rio if they don't have any treaty to extradite that robber Biggs back to Britain?' I began to waver. 'Can they?'

He poured himself a large gin with ice and shrugged.

'Want to stay and take that chance?'

I was defiant. 'If they got me back there a whole regiment of Guardsmen would storm the prison and get me out!'

'That's just what we want to avoid. Sergeant Miller, get the hell out of here! And that's an order.' I left on the plane that night. The wheels of Barbadian justice ground slowly on their bearings and finally came clean of the axles. Scotland Yard went home empty-handed once again. Ronnie was returned to Rio, to a hero's welcome and the kidnap-proof status of full Brazilian citizenship.

As I sat in the departure lounge of Grantley Adams International Airport, a posse of pressmen descended on me, grudgingly polite but spiteful that not one of them had got the real world exclusive 'hold the front page' scoop. One of them asked me, 'Well, John. You have really pulled it off. You'll never do better than this ever again in your career. What can you possibly do to top this?' I wasn't really thinking. I was too busy scanning the horizon for approaching Brazilians clutching warrants and subpoenas. I tossed it out quite casually. 'Give me a break, guys. I need some rest and relaxation and then I'll capture Josef Mengele . . . or Lord Lucan.' I should have known by then that these bastards never forget a boast, idle or otherwise.

Lucan

The woman who fell in through the door of the saloon bar of the Plumbers' Arms in Belgravia was hysterical and dripping blood all over the place. The Plumbers' Arms might sound like a kinda tough dive bar, but it's actually one of the poshest little pubs in London. It's one of the local bars near Buckingham Palace, although I don't suppose the Queen or Philip drops in very often for a large gin. It's mainly Palace staff who hang about the place. And they're quite used to the lords and ladies and dukes and duchesses who live in the mansions all around coming in for a beer and a packet of crisps.

But the night Lady Veronica Lucan lurched up to the bar, in November 1974, it obviously wasn't a social occasion. Her face was badly ripped and there were great lumps missing from her scalp. She was screaming, 'Help me, help me! I've just escaped from a murderer ... my children, my children ... he's in the house ... he's murdered the nanny.'

The landlord called the police, Veronica was piled into an ambulance and off to hospital. Two patrol cops were sent to her house a few yards away in the same street. They found the Lucan kids, unhurt but terrified. And they found a US Mail bag in the basement. Inside was the nanny, Sandra Rivett. She'd been battered to death.

In the casualty ward, Veronica was giving the eye witness detail which should have made it an open and shut case for Scotland Yard. She'd seen whodunnit. It was her husband, professional gambler John Bingham, Lord 'Lucky' Lucan. Lady Lucan said that Sandra should have had the night off to go out with her boyfriend but had stayed in with her and the kids. They had been watching TV together until Sandra went to the kitchen in the basement to make a pot of tea. When she didn't return Veronica went down to see what was keeping her.

In the basement she was jumped on from behind by a guy who whacked her on the head, tried to gouge out her eyes and choke her to death. Well-bred English girls don't give up without a fight. She got a helluva grip on his balls and squeezed until he backed off in agony. Then she turned round and saw it was her estranged husband John. He was babbling, moaning that Sandra had been killed in mistake for Lady Lucan.

The police went straight round to check Lucan's flat only 300 yards from the family home and found his clothes and cheque book, his car keys and passport still securely tucked away at home. Meanwhile his mother, the Dowager Duchess turned up at the scene of the crime and said she'd just had a phone call from Lucky Lucan. She said her son told her he'd been passing Veronica's home and seen an intruder attacking someone in the basement. When he'd gone to help the intruder had fought past him and escaped. And then Veronica had turned up and got the wrong idea that Lucky had been the killer.

Within hours of the murder, Lucan had contacted a number of friends and maintained his innocence. Then he vanished into thin air. The borrowed car he had been using was found in a seaside town on the English Channel and inside was a piece of the lead pipe used to kill the nanny. But no trace was ever found of Lucan. The theories were that he had used his network of aristocratic and gambling contacts to vanish into hiding. Or that he had committed suicide rather than face the shame of a court appearance. Or that he had actually hired the hitman who killed the nanny by mistake. And then the hitman had later killed Lucan because he didn't want the conscience-stricken Earl going to the police and dropping everyone in it. Whatever happened, the trail went cold.

At the inquest on Sandra Rivett the coroner had no doubts. He named Lord Lucan as the murderer. But that never solved anything. Lucan is still listed among the members of the famous St Moritz Toboggan Club, although he's not been seen on the slopes of the Cresta Run for years. He's still listed in Debrett's, the handbook of the British aristocracy. And his son, now grown up, has still not been allowed to inherit his father's title. The Lucan Affair is still unfinished business and it has become a sort of Quest for the Holy Grail as far as Fleet Street reporters are concerned. The poor chap has turned into a Loch Ness Monster or Abominable Snowman. On a dull news day the papers still report sightings of Lord Lucan from Patagonia to Prague.

I had made a study of the case after I had first proposed to Stephen Bentinck that we could put Executive Security on the map by pulling off a spectacular international arrest. But we could have blown our entire budget on research just trying to establish if Lucan was alive or dead. So naturally we had plumped for Ronnie Biggs. I would have gone for Lucan, or I would still go, if only somebody would give me the glimmer of a decent lead on where he is hiding – if he is even still alive. But I have memorised his face, his physical characteristics, details of his foreign bank accounts. Travelling extensively as I do, I'd hate to be sitting in the bar of an airport transit lounge and then suddenly identify the face of the guy who had been sitting at the next table and left fifteen minutes before.

At my final airport press conference after the snatch of Biggs, I had told the press that I was considering making

Lucan my next target. That was mainly in the fond hope that someone with inside information might be tempted to contact me and put me on the right track. That didn't happen, but the press never let me forget. Any time I popped up for a beer in a bar in London or New York or Los Angeles, they hounded me and waved their cheque books under my nose. It was becoming a bit of an embarrassment, so every time I was cornered by a scoop-hungry newsman, I always hinted that I was getting closer and closer to the elusive Lucan and that I was more than ready to do an exclusive deal. I must have promised the Lord Lucan exclusive to a dozen different newsmen in a dozen different bars. Whichever reporter just happened to track me down at that particular time was the one who would get the story. They thrust their business cards and private ex-directory telephone numbers on me and I tossed them in the wastebins the moment I left the bar.

At that time, in 1984, I was keeping out of the limelight anyway. After the Biggs snatch I had slipped back into the music business, running a country and western club just north of Los Angeles and helping to build a new recording studio in Memphis. To keep my hand in, I still did some investigation and security assignments for special friends, and that's what took me to Hollywood for a meeting with a movie studio executive I'll call Irving.

Irving was having a bit of a problem with some rascally distributors in Trinidad who owed him a lot of money. They hadn't been paying their bills and they had been ripping him off with wholesale piracy of his movies and videos. They had been pulling the same stunt with other film and video distributors as well and they were quite prepared to go bankrupt rather than settle with all their creditors. Irving wasn't willing to write it off as a bad debt, although he had tried a combination of threats and legal action without success. Eventually the lawyers for the Trinidad fraudsters had agreed that they would pay

164

$250,000 in an unofficial out-of-court settlement, but Irving still didn't trust them.

And there was an element of urgency and secrecy. Irving didn't want to be just one of a group of creditors who would have to settle for a few cents in the dollar. He wanted his full whack before any of the other creditors got their money. He asked me to go to Trinidad to collect the cash. He was offering an all-expenses-paid trip and a generous commission of 10 per cent.

I went to see Irving in his office on Sunset Boulevard. I took on the job and he arranged to have my flight tickets and hotel bookings organised by his own travel agent straight away. I went off to enjoy a warm English beer a short distance from Irving's office, at the Cock and Bull tavern.

The Cock and Bull is a Mecca for most British ex-pats in Los Angeles. It was almost inevitable that as soon as my eyes were accustomed to the blackness inside after the brilliant LA sunshine, the first person I recognised was one of Fleet Street's most persistent and boozy freelance hacks. His eyes, bloodshot though they were, spotted me right away and he bounded over to the bar to join me.

'Hey, John! How are things? What are you doing in LA? Who are you working for? It's Lord Lucan, isn't it?'

It was the routine friendly banter, so I said, 'Yeah, I've been told he's working disguised as a Mexican gardener at Rod Stewart's house in Beverly Hills.'

The hack wasn't to be put off.

'Like hell he is. He's hiding in Venezuela, but I suppose you already know that.'

I had some time to spare, I'd given Irving's travel agent the number of the Cock and Bull to call me with my travel details and I didn't want to have to move to another bar and miss my phone call. So I stayed for a while and the hack, who was going through a rough time with his bank and his landlord extracted the usual promise from me. I assured him, as I always did to all reporters, that I was closing in on Lord Lucan and that he would be the first to be tipped off, exclusively, as soon as I had located my quarry. It wasn't very long before the barman came over and asked me to take a phone call. I slid along the bar. It was Irving's travel agent. I grabbed a memo pad from beside the cash register and scribbled down the details.

When I finished my beer, I walked back over to my stool beside the hack and settled my bar tab. The hack was drunkenly curious.

'D'you have to go?' he asked.

I raised my right hand and tapped my index finger against my nose. 'I'm closing in on Lord Lucan, remember? Gotta rush now, I've got a lead to follow up.' I thought little more about it. A couple of hours later I was on a plane to Miami, where I switched to a flight for Port of Spain, Trinidad, and checked myself into the Hilton Hotel.

Next morning I went to see the lawyers for the people who owed my client money. Irving was right. They were jerking us around. They grinned their wide Caribbean grins at me and produced a bottle of rum and a receipt for me to sign for $250,000. 'I wanna see the money before I sign anything,' I told them.

'Hey man, it's cool,' the lawyer said. He was lounging back in his chair, fanning himself with a sheaf of threatening letters from Irving, his hideously outdated kipper tie undone way below his shirt collar.

'The money,' I repeated. 'Let me see it. Then I sign. Then I have a drink with you. Then I thank you and I leave.'

He went to the safe, pulled out an attaché case, swivelled it round on top of his desk and opened it. It was stuffed with cash. Trinidadian dollars. I leaned forward and tightened up the knot of his tie by a few inches. 'We want to see banknotes with the faces of American Presidents on them. Not Mickey Mouse money. Now I'm here because I'm British and we're all good brothers in the Commonwealth and we're both civilised people. But if you don't get me good, old-fashioned US currency, Irving is going to send some people who aren't British to enter into some discussions with you. Now these people might be Italian for all I know and they don't feel any ties of Commonwealth brotherhood. Do I have to phone Irving and tell him you'd sooner deal with Miami Italians than a fellow subject of the Queen?'

I've got to give the guy full marks for trying. 'You can take this to Florida and change it there,' he said. 'Or you'll have to wait a week for me to change it for American dollars.'

I thrust my face into his and said: 'You've got seventy-two hours. Then I pull out and a couple of collectors called Cesare and Fabrizio take over.' I left the office, caught a cab back to my hotel and called Irving.

'Keep the pressure on him, John,' Irving said. 'But nothing too heavy. I don't want the word to leak out until I've got my cash then the vultures can squabble over what's left.'

'I think he's going round his friendly dope dealers right now, Irving, and paying way over the odds on the black market to get real dollars. I've warned him you'll send in the Mob if he doesn't pay the money over to me.'

Irving chuckled. 'I thought of using them, John, but they charge five times your commission rate and they cause real bad publicity. That's the last thing I want. You take care now.'

I lay on the bed and wondered how long it would take the kipper-tie lawyer to launder the money. Then the phone rang. I knew from the faint crackle on the line it wasn't local, probably Irving calling me back. It was Los Angeles all right. It was the LA hack.

'You've found him, haven't you?' he yelled down the phone.

'Found who?' I spluttered.

'Lord Lucan.'

'What the hell are you talking about? How the hell did you know I was here?'

For all I knew the hack had eavesdropped on the call at the Cock and Bull or done the old trick of running a pencil over the impression I'd left on the second page of the memo pad at the bar.

'I'd to phone half the hotels in the island before I found you. I was right all along, it's Venezuela, isn't it?'

'Venezuela my arse, this is Trinidad!'

'Yeah, but you're only a spit away from the coast of Venezuela, aren't you? Listen, John, this is the story of the century. We can share a fortune on this one. I'm going to get some money promised by a syndication agent and I'll be on the next plane.'

That was the last thing I needed. A Lord Lucan circus hitting the headlines while I'm supposed to be quietly collecting Irving's money. So I pleaded with him.

'Just give me a couple of days. I can't get to Lucan just yet. You're right, it's Venezuela, but he's travelling down from Caracas to a village on the coast. This is top secret. Keep it to yourself for another couple of days, till I'm ready to move and I'll call you. The story's all yours, absolutely exclusive, we just don't want to blow it at this stage.' I lied the best I could. And so did he. He promised me my secret was safe with him. He swore on his mother's life and his children's eyesight. Then he called New York, and New York called London. And London called Glasgow.

The next call I got was from my old friend the Scottish journalist Gavin Goodwin, the man who caused the disastrous leak which cost me all that money in my first attempt to snatch Ronnie Biggs. 'John, you've got to let me in on this one,' he pleaded. 'There will be no slip-ups this time. I can get you the best price and the biggest publicity ever. Trust me, trust me.'

I asked him: 'Gavin, where did you get this information?'

He said quite casually: 'We bought the tip-off from a freelance in Los Angeles.'

I often wonder if the LA hack's mother was struck dead that night or his children went blind but I don't suppose God is dumb enough to take a reporter's promise at face value. I gave the same spiel to Gavin about giving me a couple of days and Gavin was on the next plane to Trinidad. Within a few hours he was joined by a back-up team from New York. And my reputation for discretion and low-key operations was about to go out of the window.

I gathered them all in my hotel room and told them, 'Two of my men are meeting Lord Lucan in a village in Venezuela, just across the horizon. We have some business to conduct with him and then I'll deliver him to you.'

I knew already that they were trying to bribe the hotel switchboard staff to monitor my calls and check on any outgoing or incoming telex messages, so I'd done a bit of bribing of my own and sent myself fake telex messages from non-existent accomplices to back up my story. And I got one frantic coded call from the Port of Spain kipper-tie lawyer. The money was ready.

I got a cab to his office and came back to the hotel to pick up my things. I took the reporters into my room and opened the brand new attaché case. Inside was US $250,000, in used notes. Their eyes were popping out of their sockets. 'This is why Lucan is coming to meet me,' I explained. 'I have become a courier for one of his wealthy gambling contacts in London who keeps him supplied with money. When Lucky Lucan comes to collect this lot, his luck will have run out. Be patient, he is almost within your grasp. I have to meet him in a village about sixty miles inland from the Venezuelan coast. There is a Brazilian warrant out for my arrest after the Biggs kidnap. I have to sail to Venezuela on a fishing boat and sneak past any police patrols. You've got to understand that I'd never make it if I took you guys with me. It would look like the D-Day landings. If you give me your word you will stay put in the hotel and maintain tight security, I'll capture Lucan and bring him to the coast and you can sail over and get your story.' They agreed, reluctantly and impatiently.

I got a cab down to the fishing port and made some indiscreet inquiries about renting a fishing boat to sail the twenty or so miles across the Gulf of Paria, through the waters the native fishermen call the Mouth of the Dragon. The locals do the trip all the time. There was no shortage of takers. In case the reporters checked up on me, the word was out that I was making the trip.

Then I simply caught a bus to the airport and a flight to Miami. I deposited the money in a bank, called Irving, deducted my commission and spent a pleasant two days at a hotel in Coconut Grove, idly wondering how long the patient reporters would wait in Port of Spain. I started to brood about it. They had almost ruined that job for me. This could happen every time I tried to do a confidential assignment. There would always be reporters wanting to chase headlines, and to put me on the front pages. One way to get them off my back was actually to find Lord Lucan. Or there was another way. I flew back to Trinidad.

I walked into the Hilton hotel, brushing my hands wildly against my thighs and cursed: 'My God, the leeches, the snakes, it's sheer hell over there.' Then I outlined my plan. 'We have Lord Lucan. Two of my men have got him tied up in a jungle hut near the coast. First thing in the morning we set off to sail there. Now, I've fixed it with a local boat skipper and we want to make this look like a tourist fishing trip. So, no passports, no credit cards,

170

no large amounts of cash. It's just a cheap day's outing.
When we cross the Dragon's Mouth, we set down on the
beach and I take you to Lord Lucan. We can be in and out
in a matter of hours.'

They agreed. They could hardly wait for daybreak.

My plan was quite simple. It was going to cost me a few
hundred bucks but it would be well worth it. I would take
this press party, with no passports, i.d. or money, enter
Venezuela illegally with them, march them a mile into
the jungle, give them the slip and sail back to Trinidad.
Let them talk their way out of that when the local police
came across them. I knew they would find civilisation in a
little town called Guiria, only about ten miles from the
landing spot I had chosen. They might even spend a few
uncomfortable nights in the local jail there. But it would
teach them not to put their noses in where they weren't
wanted. I figured they might leave me alone after that.
And just like the first attempt to trap Ronnie Biggs, the
plan went wrong. Why? The same reason as before. Fleet
Street reporters gossip.

A few hours before we were due to set off, I got a call
in my room from Gerry Brown, the freelance who had
been right in the thick of things on the successful Biggs
snatch. He was calling from London. 'You double-crossing
bastard, Miller,' he growled at me. 'You've got Lord
Lucan and you never gave me a sniff of it.'

'Shit, who told you that?'

'Damn near everybody in Fleet Street knows about it.'

It was getting out of hand. I warned him gently, 'Gerry,
don't come out here, you'd be wasting your time.'

'Don't bullshit me, John. It'll be front page news before
the night is out and I'm booked on the next flight.'

That was it. Gerry was working for a rival paper to
Gavin's outfit. Gerry had been straight with me when I
gave him the Biggs exclusive and I didn't want to have to
lead him down the jungle path with the others. Besides, if

the story was breaking in the first editions in London that night, Trinidad was going to be swamped with hacks the next day and I would have needed to charter the *Queen Mary* to get my revenge on all of them.

Anyway Gerry's call gave me the perfect excuse to give a tongue-lashing to Gavin's team, without me losing any face. 'You loose-lipped bastards have done it again,' I stormed at them. 'Your fucking security is a shambles. Now the whole world knows what I'm up to. There's no way I'm going into Venezuela to get captured because of you lot. You've blown the biggest story of your careers and you've only got yourselves to blame.' There was a stunned silence. I had no idea how Gerry had got on to the story and I didn't care. Gavin and his mates were white-faced. They had been a wee bit frightened by my outburst and mock rage. And they would face one of the biggest inquests in the history of their newspaper into how word of their exclusive had leaked out to their deadly rivals.

It was a good result for me. Honour had been satisfied. Next morning I went to the airport just as swarms from the *Daily Express* and the *Daily Mail* and every other damned daily and Sunday in London poured off the plane carrying copies of the *Mirror* and *Star* with the banner headlines 'I've Got Lord Lucan, Claims Biggs Kidnapper!'

I barged through passport and immigration control, cussing at everyone in my path and shouted my way on to the Miami flight. The plane took off and I locked myself in the toilet cubicle and laughed and laughed until the tears rolled down my cheeks. I'd had my revenge on all of them, and they thought they'd blown it themselves. Now they'd never know if I really had found Lord Lucan or not. They would be tormented with doubt and forever cursing themselves. I would emerge as the true professional, screwed up by the amateurs of Fleet Street. I had evened up the score with them. I should have known better.

*　　*　　*

The Lucan bandwagon had gained a lot more passengers, and it turned round from Trinidad and rumbled north to Miami. When I got off the plane the advance party had got there before me. There was a scrum of TV spotlights, cameras, notebooks, tape-recorders. I was hemmed in. Ambushed. Then this bearded guy stepped through the crowd and said, 'Hi, John, you don't know me but we've got mutual friends. If you want to get away from this pack I've got a car right outside. Just jump in.'

I got into a car and the first thing I saw was a bloody press photographer. Malcolm Balfour, a South African who lives in Florida and syndicates photos around the world. Surprise, surprise! Miller's been taken for a ride. Literally. But there was something about my 'kidnapper' which stopped me jumping straight out of the car. It turned out he wasn't just any old opportunist. He was Colin Harrington, better known to the readers of titillating British newspapers as Colin Levy, ex-husband of Norma Levy.

About the same time as Lord Lucan went missing, Norma Levy nearly brought down the Tory government. She was a high-class hooker whose clients included the Army Minister, Lord Lambton. Now, Colin is never a man to turn his back on a quick buck, so he had trotted off to Fleet Street with this information and the *News of the World* newspaper hid one of their photographers in a wardrobe in the bedroom, equipped with a two-way mirror, and they got the pictures to prove it. But they handed the negatives back to Colin, never paid him a penny and published the story anyway. It was a wonderful juicy scandal and the great British newspaper readership could hardly believe its luck.

Two great stories hot on the heels of each other. First, Lord Lucan, aristocrat and drunken gambler, vanishes after his nanny is beaten to death, and now another lordship, a cabinet minister, is caught in bed with a whore. Booming circulation figures are built on such earth-shattering events. The Levys had come under so much pressure that they'd fled the country without Fleet Street fulfilling any of its promises of cash in return for exclusive details of the scandal. Colin was now divorced from Norma. He'd married an American girl whose parents owned Rich Airways, a little cargo-passenger outfit operating out of Miami. They had a beautiful house in Coral Gables, and that's where Colin took me.

When we got there I asked Colin to send Malcolm Balfour away, so we could talk privately. I figured Colin had no great love for reporters, so I levelled with him. And he laughed almost as hard as I did. 'Can you do me a favour, Colin?' I asked. 'My wife is being pestered like hell at home in Memphis and I'd like to stay here for a few days until the dust settles.' He agreed quite happily and when the press finally tracked me down to Colin's house, he answered their calls on the phone and at the door and told them to piss off. They had all been left with egg on their faces – but still some of them refused to believe it.

That's when Colin said to me, 'John, this is just too good to let it go at this. They're just begging for more punishment. We could have a lot more fun with them.'

There had never been any real hard evidence that I had ever located Lord Lucan but one persistent outfit that wouldn't take no for an answer was the Independent Television News crew from Washington. Their reporter John Suchet kept sticking notes in Colin's letter-box, his film crew dogged us everywhere we went. Worse than that, Suchet was trying to force a fee of £5,000 into our hands just for a brief film clip of Lucan.

It was Colin's idea. 'They want Lord Lucan, we'll give them Lord Lucan,' he said. 'Please, John, I feel the British media owes me a debt as well. And I want to rub their noses in it just as much as you do.' He went on to explain his plan. He could rent a seaworthy cruiser and he had a few buddies who could always be counted on to play a part in an elaborate practical joke. He'd take us to a deserted beach and one of his men would play the part of Lord Lucan.

I've never been one to knock a good joke but I said to him, 'No, enough is enough. It's better to leave them wondering. Besides it stops being a joke if we take Suchet's five grand and set him up for a swindle. I don't want any part of that.'

Colin was anxious to placate me. 'No, no, John. We don't take a penny off them. That would be a criminal con. No, just go along with me. We'll do it at my expense just to give me a bit of satisfaction.'

I thought about it. I wasn't entirely sure exactly what Colin had in mind. But it would be a useful ploy to break the siege of newsmen who had lost my trail and were giving my wife Sarah a hard time at home in Memphis. So that's when we decided to take Suchet and his team on a magical mystery tour off the coast of Florida.

We all went to Fort Lauderdale where Colin chose a thirty-footer for our trip. And the man from ITN insisted on paying for the charter. Colin shrugged. Fair enough if they wanted to dig into their own pockets to buy the custard pie we were going to throw into their faces, let them do it.

Since he was picking up the tab, John Suchet thought he'd try to dictate the terms. He wanted to know exactly where we were going and when we would get there. I told him we had transferred Lucan to a desert island in the Gulf of Mexico but that we would have to keep radio silence until we got there to prevent anyone listening in to our frequency tracking us down. He agreed after throwing a little tantrum and called his office in London.

I had worked out a simple code. He could radio map co-ordinates through to his office when we reached the island, but the figures for our position would be reversed. In other words 1234 would become 4321. Quite basic, but it added a hilarious air of intrigue to our mission. And we had one unsuspecting ally with us, Malcolm Balfour, the local freelance. Malcolm wasn't in on the joke, but he was earning a fat fee from ITN for his services.

I stowed a few items of kit on board, and we set off. On the second day out, I still couldn't believe we were going to pull it off. Colin had carefully navigated us in circles between Fort Lauderdale and our 'desert' island, Key Largo, about eighty miles down the coast. Colin was muttering darkly about avoiding Guatemalan coast-guard patrols and we never once lost sight of the glow of the lights of downtown Miami just over the horizon. The daylight hours were only disturbed by the constant whine of aircraft overhead, lining up for the final approach to Miami International, and still the newsmen never noticed.

We planned to keep it up for another day or so. Colin and I were quite enjoying the cruise. But on the second day, Suchet was sun-bathing on the deck and he glanced through a hatch and saw me checking some of my equipment. A Colt .45 and a bullet-proof jacket to be exact. He freaked out. 'I want to radio my office.'

I calmed him down and said he could do that in a few hours, and I nodded for Colin to swing the boat towards Key Largo. When the time came, I gave him a set of navigation co-ordinates which would have put us somewhere between Cuba and the Yucatan Peninsula, about two hundred and fifty miles away from our true position. He radioed them through. I could hear the reply come back on the ship to shore radio. The guy said: 'Very funny, John. That puts you at the North Pole.'

Suchet went white with fear. 'You're going to kill us and take our money. You're mad! I've got a wife and two children. I don't want to die!' He was supposed to be an experienced, hardened journalist, but he wouldn't have lasted five minutes as a new recruit at the Guards' depot. I told him to stop snivelling. I'd given him a real set of co-ordinates for the southern Gulf of Mexico but his people had goofed at the other end. The message he'd passed on about the code, simple though it was, had obviously become garbled.

Then I remembered Malcolm Balfour spoke Afrikaans. 'I'll tell you what I'll do,' I said, 'I'll let Malcolm call his wife in Florida and tell her in Afrikaans to get in touch with your people in Washington and give them the map reference in the clear, with no coding.' That seemed to satisfy him.

We stalled a little further, so that there wasn't much daylight left when we reached the jetty at Key Largo. There was a line of palm trees above the tidemark on the beach, and the wreckage of a small sailboat in the sand. Beside the wreckage were a few bleached white scattered bones. Don't ask me where they came from but they had a powerfully unsettling effect on the intrepid TV news crew. And there was, thank God, a good surf running against the beach, because just on the other side of the line of palms was the bloody Transocean Causeway and the noise of the traffic was almost deafening.

Colin went ashore and met our 'Lord Lucan', one of his mates called Pete, just off the highway. It was the usual humid, damp Florida night and Pete was having a bit of trouble keeping his five-dollar joke-shop moustache stuck to his upper lip. But now the scene was set. I slipped below decks when no one was looking, dipped my hand into a small tin of camouflage cream and then strapped myself into my bullet-proof jacket.

Back on deck the TV crew rigged up a radio microphone to my pristine new flak jacket. And we waited and then waited some more. I strapped the Colt .45 to my hip and did something I never do. I lit a cigarette. That was the signal. A tall figure with a moustache stepped out of the palm trees about a hundred and fifty yards away. Everyone held their breath as I eased myself slowly from the boat and walked towards him.

Pete played his part beautifully. We had a brief argument and Pete pulled a gun on me. It was full of blanks, but I still made damned sure he wasn't even pointing it in my direction when he loosed off a round. The TV spotlights burst into life. I tumbled backwards and as Pete ran through the palms, I fired ten shots in the air after him. My bullets were for real.

I dragged myself back to our boat to find mass hysteria everywhere. Poor Malcolm Balfour. I never knew he wore a wig. And when the gunshots had started he'd jumped over the side of our launch with all his camera gear. Worse than that, his wig came off and floated away briskly on the Gulf Stream. It's probably on a beach in Galway by now.

The TV crew were whining in distress for us to get the hell out of it. So we roared off with the engines screaming. And when the sound recordist came down below to take the radio microphone off my flak jacket, he reeled back in horror. There was a smouldering hole just above my heart. I ripped the jacket off, moaning, and he nearly passed out when he saw the massive black and blue bruising on my ribs. I cursed him and crawled out on to the deck and the darkness.

There was a shocked and stunned silence on the way home that night, with the engines at full throttle and Colin still having to twist the boat in circles to pretend we were covering a great distance instead of just cruising back along the coast to Fort Lauderdale. Suchet was crouched over a portable TV monitor, running and re-running the video tape of the shoot-out and muttering to himself, 'We could all have been killed.'

Me? I just lay on deck marvelling at how the lighted tip of a cigarette can burn a hole in a flak jacket just like a bullet strike and how a quick smear of camo cream on your chest can look like bruised and broken ribs.

Suchet couldn't wait to get off the boat in Fort Lauderdale and film a dramatic reconstruction of the Lord Lucan encounter. He even bought a flak jacket, tied it to a palm tree and fired a .32 into it. And blow me if it didn't make a smouldering hole just like a cigarette burn: Suchet told the whole world it was conclusive proof that I had actually been struck by a bullet. Still, they were just seeing what they wanted to see.

Colin and I had a rollicking farewell drink, together with our own Lord Lucan, Pete, and I smiled all the way home to Memphis. But Colin Harrington had more than just his revenge on meddlesome media men. He knew that in the dog-eat-dog world of British journalism, there is no love lost between newspapers and their television rivals. He waited until ITN screened their world-wide exclusive footage of the Lord Lucan shoot-out and the TV executives were patting each other on the back, and praising John Suchet for his fearless, dynamic reporting. Then Colin phoned the reporter at the *News of the World* who had stiffed him for his payment on the story of his ex-wife, the hooker, and Lord Lambton. And he offered to sell him the story of our little stunt.

Colin had made sure he never took a penny of ITN's £5,000 to set up the hoax. But he cheerfully took £10,000 from the *News of the World* for exposing how it was done. And he took most of the credit, or blame, himself. I suppose you've got to admire the bloody man's nerve!

Bhagwash

You could say that mysticism is not my bag. I mean if I am going to spend time sitting around I'd rather be on a high stool with a stiff drink than in the lotus position with a low-fat yoghurt. When it comes to bizarre religious sects, the only thing I will say is that they do seem to attract some really gorgeous girls and they do seem to have a less than puritanical attitude towards sex. Which was the little problem I walked into one day in 1984: the Beauty Queen and the Bhagwan.

I have acquired something of a reputation for oddball assignments over the years so it was no great surprise when I got a phone call from this contact of mine in Miami. He was acting on behalf of a friend of his – a rich, self-made businessman he called Jack. Jack had this beautiful daughter who had joined up with a cult of weirdos who worshipped a little bearded chap called Bhagwan Shree Rajneesh.

He'd attracted a lot of attention over the years as well as the nickname 'Bhagwash'. What made people sit up and take notice was that this fakir fellow not only seemed to have amazing mystic powers over the fairer sex, he also had a most unascetic interest in hard cash and the trappings of millionaire life. He particularly liked Rolls-Royces. Not just one Roller, he had a whole fleet of them, garaged on his land up in Oregon. He and his gang had moved there after he'd abandoned the ashram in Poona which had become infamous as a sort of knocking shop for rich and aristocratic hippies.

To the considerable disgust of the local inhabitants, the Bhagwash and his followers were establishing a new Oregon city called Rajneeshpuram and they were doing it in a very tough and unholy fashion. They were armed and they were playing politics. In fact it sounded more like a Mafia operation than a mission by born-again Buddhists.

Needless to say, Jack was none too happy about this. He didn't want his little girl being caught up in a mad remake of the Jonestown holy suicide massacre. About a week before I got the call Jack's daughter had made a call of her own. It was the first time she'd talked to her father in years. She rabbited away about this and that, inquired after his golf handicap, wished him a happy birthday, though she was a month or so late, and Jack sensed she was scared of something, afraid to say what was on her mind. He thought she had the feeling the phone was being tapped.

It sounded like a fun job so I said I'd fly down to Miami and have a chat with Jack. He had quite a ritzy pad: you couldn't get through the gates without talking into a squawk box. Everything was electronically operated. He had his own private waterway with a sixty-foot power boat. Big house. Nice garden. Filipino servants. Not exactly Bhagwash league but he was all right, Jack. Well, he'd done all right but I wasn't too sure he *was* all right. He had mean, piggy eyes and a paunch under an alligator shirt. All in all he was a mean-looking bastard.

'OK,' he said, 'how much do you know?'

'Enough to be here,' I said.

'Will you do it?'

'Let's get one thing straight,' I said. 'Nothing illegal. I'll do what I can, but in the USA I'm not into clever-clever stuff with guns and drugs and all that. I have to stay legal.'

'No problem,' said Jack, and I was very aware of those piggy eyes. 'In any case Cathy can't be forced. She's like her old man. You force her to do something and she'll turn round and do the exact opposite.'

'So all you want me to do is to go up to Oregon and make nice with everyone? Talk reasonably to Cathy. Say her dad's been missing her.' Piggy eyes said yes.

It sounded dead easy, but it wasn't. The Bhagwash had turned his security operations over to his own goon squad. And they were a heavy mob. Not the IRA, I grant you, but they knew the basics. There was no way I could take them on single-handed without a bit of subtlety. I couldn't just go in with a hand gun and take her out. They'd had trouble already with the press, with infiltrators, with local rednecks. They controlled the little airstrip in the local town of Antelope with an iron hand. They had the place sewn up.

'Tell you what,' I said, 'if I get in there and talk to her and she doesn't want to come back, that'll cost you five grand. That'll cover my expenses. But if I persuade her to come home to Daddy, then that's twenty-five grand.'

I was going to have to pretend to be an eager young Bhagwash recruit. That wasn't easy for an old bruiser like me. And the Bhagwash people were armed and trigger happy. If I screwed up I could end up dead in a ditch. Jack obviously wasn't short of a bob or two. I reckoned twenty-five grand was a reasonable price for a daughter. At first Jack seemed a bit reluctant, but he didn't argue too seriously. 'I'm not going to haggle over a few lousy thousand,' he said. 'Cathy's my only child.'

I didn't much like Jack. And the thought did cross my mind that she might be no better off with him than the Bhagwash. But he was her father and twenty-five grand was twenty-five grand. 'I'll do it,' I said.

'Good,' said Jack. 'What do you need?'

I'd taken the precaution of reading up a couple of

magazine articles in the local library. Not that I admitted that, of course. I wanted to give the impression of being super well-informed. 'My contacts have warned me not to take these people too lightly,' I said. 'The inside gen is that they're into more than stringing beads and chanting mantras. You have to give them the same sort of respect you'd give the Mafia or the PLO. If your daughter does agree to come out, we'll need to get out in a hurry. I'm not hanging around waiting for a Greyhound bus.'

'You want an escape vehicle?'

'I mean I want a helicopter. Plus pilot.'

'Sure, I can fix that.' He didn't bat an eyelid. 'I'll give you a phone number. The guy's done jobs for me before. He's reliable. What else?'

'Information,' I said. 'When did she join this circus? And why? Drugs? Boyfriend trouble? Or is she just missing a screw or two?'

Not much help there. The phone call from Cathy had been the first communication he'd had from her in four years.

'Do you have a picture?'

He handed over the framed photo on his desk. It was hinged in the middle like a book. One side was empty. The other showed a pretty girl with short hair and a fringe, perfect teeth and a string of pearls. She looked almost too prim and proper to be true. My guess was drugs.

'When was this taken?'

'Four years ago, when she was twenty-one.'

'Nothing more recent?'

''Fraid not.'

'Height?'

He waved his hands indecisively around his chest and chin. 'She comes up to about here on me,' he said. That was a huge help.

'You sure you haven't got any other pictures?' I wanted

184

a snap, not a studio portrait. I needed something with some reference points that would help me determine her build. I'd learned some shorthand tricks of the trade in the military – a house brick is two and a half inches tall plus a half inch of mortar; a pillar box is five foot five. Put a person against either and you could judge their height to within half an inch. Not that Jack was likely to have a photo of Cathy alongside a pillar box or a brick wall. He didn't. The studio picture was the only one.

'Distinguishing marks?' I asked. 'Scars? Any little gestures or affectations? Does she stutter, lisp? Does she pronounce any words funny?' He was useless. Nothing.

'I'd know Cathy anywhere,' he said, lamely. Which didn't help me a whole lot.

So I made him write a personal letter full of little details which only she would know. It had to be 100 per cent authentic. And I gave him a strip of passport photos I'd had taken at the airport. He signed across them. That way she'd know I was authentic too.

I didn't want to spend too long on this job. Twenty-four hours to find a place to put the chopper down, mark the spot so it could be seen from the air and phone through a map reference to the pilot. Today was Wednesday. If I flew there tonight from Miami, I could scout round and penetrate Rajneeshpuram on Saturday; allow a day or two to find Cathy and then give her the sales pitch. Then we'd see what happened.

'A week today,' I said, when Jack had finished writing. 'We'll RV at Portland Airport next Wednesday. OK?'

He shook his head. 'I'll send my sister,' he said. 'I don't want to get involved. As long as Cathy's out of the place, she can do what she likes. I've done trying to tell her what to do. I just want her out of there.'

I had a lucky break at Portland Airport as soon as I arrived. American airports are often crawling with

cranks of all descriptions. Every imaginable sect has a
representative in the terminal building, unfathomable
tracts in one hand and begging bowls in the other.
Naturally the Bhagwash had a man in place: bearded
bloke, red-dyed T-shirt, jeans, Bhagwhan literature,
spaced-out expression, open palm.

I went over to the news-stand and pretended to glance
through the magazines. Sure enough, he recognised a
sucker when he saw one. 'Excuse me,' he said.

'Not at all.'

'Now,' he said, 'you're English. What brings you here?'

'Scottish, actually,' I corrected him. 'I'm just travelling
around, sort of at a loose end.'

'Ah, yes,' he nodded understandingly. 'We are all on the
road looking for happiness. Is what you're doing working
for you?'

I shook my head and tried to look sad and vulnerable.
'Happiness still seems an awful long way away,' I said.

He seemed pleased with this. 'I have a feeling about
you,' he said. I had a feeling about him too, but I bit my
tongue.

'Brother,' he said, producing this fat volume, 'I'd like to
give you this. It's the thoughts and wisdom of my guru,
Bhagwan Shree Rajneesh. Before I knew Bhagwan I had
the exact same feelings which trouble you. The more
I chased happiness, the more happiness ran away from
me . . .'

I switched into a pretty good imitation of a Bhagwan
meditation trance at this point and when I snapped myself
out of it five minutes later, he was still rambling on.

'It's like trying to explain the mysteries of love,' he was
saying. 'Like the inexplicable is inexplicable. If your soul
is in torment you should turn to meditation. Maybe even
go to Rajneeshpuram and be in the Bhagwan's energy
yourself. I'd like to be there myself, but I'm here. You

know' – he gave a particularly fatuous smile – 'you are where you are,' he said.

I smiled back. If this was a sample of the Bhagwan's wisdom, I was going to have trouble keeping a straight face. 'I could just go there,' I asked, 'as a perfect stranger?'

'Friend,' he beamed, 'you may be perfect but you're no stranger.'

I had a feeling he'd used this line before but I did some more smiling and tried to look like the sort of guy who'd make good Bhagwan material. 'Where is this Rajnee Pooja?' I asked.

My mangling of the name made him laugh even more stupidly. 'Here is the brochure,' he said. 'It is the most beautiful place in the whole world. Go. You will be welcomed. You will find happiness. The Bhagwan is good. You will find happiness . . .'

Jesus, I thought. And then I remembered my promise to Jack, and the uplifting transcendental prospect of earning $25,000.

The next day, driving in a rented car from Portland to Antelope, I was inclined to agree with my bearded friend in the red T-shirt. The road wound through rugged hills, dwarfed by 11,000 feet of Mount Hood looming up on the left. There were massive pines and lush meadows of golden grass swaying in the breeze. I felt like someone in a Marlboro cigarette commercial. I'd spent the morning making preparations. At a backpacking outfitters I'd bought two maps of the Antelope area. One I sent by messenger service to the helicopter pilot, Mike. The other was in the glove compartment. I bought some tough dustbin liners and a five-gallon can which I filled with kerosene. Kerosene kills grass. This was how I intended marking my helicopter landing-spot. Now I was trying to enjoy the scenery and not worry about what could go wrong. I didn't do too well. There was an awful lot which could go wrong.

The closer I got to Antelope, the more like desert the scenery became. This part of Oregon is called the Mutton Mountains. Sheep country once, I suppose, but not any more. It's all sage-brush and juniper with a bit of wheat-grass. Every so often a tumbleweed would be blown across the road, cartwheeling along like some prickly animal. It was real outdoor country. Everyone had four-wheel-drive pickups with the obligatory gun racks and deer rifles and the drivers wore caps with the names of tractors on them. They made me feel almost sorry for the Rajneeshis. It really wasn't the sort of place to be traipsing around in magenta robes and babbling about the Inner Light.

Antelope had a population of forty. That was what the sign on the outskirts of town said. It looked just like the set of a western – a grove of cottonwoods, couple of gas stations, old general store. The main difference was that instead of cowhands and guys in boots and stetsons, the streets were swarming with people in red, orange, mauve and magenta robes. In front of the post office there were a couple of pickups. The first was a brand new Chevrolet with the community's seagull logo on the side above the words 'City of Rajneeshpuram Peace Force'. The stickers on the rear bumper read, 'Jesus Saves, Moses Invests, Bhagwan Spends' and 'Be a Joke Unto Yourself'. The second pickup was a beaten-up Dodge, dark green, red trim. There was a Winchester 95 in the gunrack and a bumper sticker, which said 'Better Dead Than Red'. As far as the local rednecks were concerned the Invasion had happened. Only it wasn't the Soviets.

The road to Rajneeshpuram was marked by marble gateposts and a sign that read, 'I go to the feet of the Awakened One'. Halfway along it was a sentry-box with two guards, a bearded man and a blonde woman. They both wore .357s in their shoulder holsters. After they had waved me through I looked in the rearview mirror and saw the woman pick up a two-way radio. The Awakened One was obviously not going to be caught napping.

I suppose it was ten miles as the crow flies from Antelope to the Bhagwan's place. The winding dirt road makes it seem at least double that. The drive took me nearly an hour and everything I drove through was the Bhagwan's land – not bad for dishing up a book of platitudes laced with sexual permissiveness. He owned about a hundred square miles. From time to time I passed maroon- and purple-clad work gangs cutting brush, drilling into the rock, moving muck with bulldozers. And every so often there was another sentry-box with armed guards.

At last I reached the crest of a long hill and saw the valley about a mile below. I pulled off the road and got out to look. The whole valley was cluttered with buildings. At one time this place had been called the Big Muddy Ranch. John Wayne had filmed *Big Muddy* and *Rooster Cogburn* there with Katharine Hepburn.

The Duke must have been spinning in his grave, his tolerance for hippie riff-raff being even lower than mine. The original ranch buildings had been lost in the architectural hotch-potch which had grown up around them. There must have been about fifty mobile homes, a bunch of prefabricated ranch houses and A-frames, barns, aeroplane hangars and tents. Tractors and pickups were moving along the dirt roads that crisscrossed the place and there were aircraft at the end of a paved landing strip.

I turned the car round and drove back down below the crest of the hill where I couldn't be observed from the valley. Then I got the maps out of the glove compartment. It wasn't hard to get my bearings. There was the ranch, there were the surrounding hills with elevations marked; there were the canyons between; there was the road to Antelope. Not far away I spotted a likely rendezvous point: it looked flat and seemed to be screened from the valley and the road by good-sized hills. I could reach it through a small canyon round the next bend in the road.

It didn't take long to drive round, then scramble up the canyon. It seemed ideal – a flat strip of caked earth, maybe a couple of hundred feet wide. Could have been an old riverbed. It was about three miles from the Bhagwan HQ and well hidden. I just hoped the helicopter arrived on time. Otherwise we'd have to hoof it across what looked like pretty rough terrain. Heading for Antelope was out of the question. The nearest safe place was a town called Madras about forty miles away. Everything in between was Bhagwan country.

I calculated that from ground level my kerosene burn would just look like dead grass. From the air it would be a big 'J' – about twenty-five feet square. Bad news if the Bhagwan's own helicopters spotted it but I couldn't do anything about that. I'd just finished pouring out the kerosene and stowing dustbin liners full of civilian get-away clothes behind a rock when a blue pickup came round the corner. There were five guys in mauve and maroon in the back, all holding Uzis. There was a girl in charge – quite sexy – T-shirt, no bra, pistol in shoulder holster. The Modesty Blaise look.

It wasn't a good moment. They were obviously suspicious. Modesty's smile was all mouth and no eyes and when she asked if I was coming down to Rajneeshpuram it felt more like an order than an invitation. An order laced with sexual promise, but an order for all that. 'Sorry,' I said. 'Prior engagement in Portland. A gentleman's word, otherwise I'd love to stay and have a chat.' For a moment I thought I was under arrest but they let me go.

'You'll be back,' she said, as I drove past. And that felt like an order too.

I called Jack's pilot from my hotel in Portland. He sounded quite competent and we arranged a rendezvous on Wednesday, one hour before sunset. If I failed to show it was the same deal Thursday. Again on Friday. If that didn't work, all bets were off and I'd be on my own. It was something to look forward to.

As usual when working, I travelled light except for the extra socks. I always wear two pairs of black socks on each foot. It's not just superstition – it's a good place to hide banknotes. If you have to take your socks off the notes stay concealed between the two layers of sock! I put $500 apiece into a couple of ziploc sandwich bags and tucked them between the socks. I also slipped a third bag of notes down the front of my underpants – a sort of financial chastity belt which I guessed might come in handy back in the land of sex and mysticism. If my friend Modesty came looking there I'd have some incentive to tell her to keep her hands off!

I took the bus to Antelope, ordered a coffee in 'Zorba the Buddha' and began to chat up a waitress in beads and a Bhagwan T-shirt. It wasn't difficult to seem like a lost soul in search of nirvana. That's what she got all the time – blokes looking for an escape from reality. As far as she was concerned this was the gateway to heaven and she was the receptionist. So when I gave her a load of bullshit about trying to give meaning to my worthless life she swallowed it hook, line and sinker and said I should hitch a lift with Swami Deva.

Swami Deva was a short fat guy with the regulation robe and shoulder holster. He was sitting in the lotus position on the bonnet of his pickup eating a piece of wholemeal pitta bread. I put on my best Robbie Burns Cock O' the North-Tam O'Shanter Scottish brogue and gave him my little-boy-lost spiel. Like the waitress he'd heard it all before. 'Climb in,' he said. Simple as that.

A few minutes later we pulled up outside an ugly prefab in downtown Rajneeshpuram. A posse of men and women in mauve hung around holding some ugly Dobermanns on short leashes. Inside, half a dozen secretaries were phoning, typing, staring at VDUs, for all the world as if they were in any capitalist typing-pool. Except they were all in red.

Two armed swamis with a Dobermann checked me out. Then they took me through to a senior swami, a burly bloke who had Vietnam Vet written all over him. He wanted to know my spiritual history. Had I ever been in any of the New Religions – transcendental meditation, Unification Church, EST? I said I was a simple country boy who'd lost his way.

He smiled. As a matter of fact they all smiled all the time, which I found extremely disconcerting. 'Welcome, brother,' he said.

Creep, I thought, and smiled straight back.

For all the peace, love and brown rice, being with the Bhagwan was a lot like being in the Army. It was more Pioneer Corps than Brigade of Guards, I grant you, but there was a uniform, barracks and mess hall – the Magdalena Dining Hall! Also I was confined to camp. Only privileged swamis were allowed into Antelope. We were all swamis – it apparently means 'master of yourself' – but some were more swami than others. There was even a regular crackle of small arms' fire from the range. Just like Caterham.

As soon as I'd been checked, my clothes were taken away to be dyed. The Bhagwan had decreed that all of his sannyasins or disciples should dress in the colours of the sunrise. As a new recruit I was assigned to a single-sex dormitory. Where, I asked myself, was all this unbridled fornication I'd been anticipating? There were between ten and fifteen of us in there. Really we were just slave labour. All possessions confiscated – no TV, no newspapers and the only books had been written by the Bhagwan. We spent the day 'worshipping', which meant working the land or listening to dirge-like music or interminable recorded Bhagwan speeches. Pure mumbo-jumbo.

The little man certainly had it made. He had a solar-heated indoor pool, a flock of white peacocks with bells strapped to their ankles and the famous fleet of Rolls-Royces, all airbrushed with psychedelic designs. Quite an airforce too – three DC-3s, a Lear jet and a Mitsubishi turbo-prop, a twin-engined Islander and a couple of choppers. I calculated that was worth about ten million dollars.

The Bhagwan owned thirty 'Zorba the Buddha' restaurants, nightclubs, hotels. People carrying shoulder-bags of loot kept scurrying in and out of the town. And the town itself was expanding almost as you watched – shopping mall, medical centre, bakery turning out 600 loaves a day, a poultry barn with 2,000 chickens guarded by emus which were supposed to be deadly when it came to killing rattlesnakes. And a population of 4,000, rising fast. At least half of them women, one of them Jack's daughter, Cathy. I had to find her fast and I'd hardly had time to look.

I spent most of the second day out in the fields. Hard work and useless. No chance to scout around and look for Cathy. It was Sunday already. The chopper was coming in on Wednesday. I was on a tight schedule and I seemed to be getting nowhere fast. The next day I opted out of worship in the fields and worshipped for real. There were about fifty of us crammed in a windowless room. Dynamic meditation, the Bhagwan called it. First we hyperventilated for ten minutes; then we did ten minutes free-form dancing; then ten minutes jumping up and down with our arms in the air shouting, 'Hoo! Hoo!' The woman in charge said this was to 'awaken the sex centre'. Not the usual way I woke my sex centre, but it takes all sorts. I was glad my old friends in the sergeants' mess couldn't see me.

After the physical jerks we watched a video on the Bhagwan talking more Bhagwash, then we had some silent contemplation, then a discussion which consisted of one dropout after another getting up and telling us how pathetic they were. Dear God! After a while I asked to be excused and went out to meditate on my own. Our leader said I could meditate anywhere I liked. 'The Bhagwan's presence makes the whole valley a Buddhafield,' he had said. I said I was glad to see it.

Outside who should I find but my Modesty Blaise friend. She was wearing salmon pink mini-shorts. Very sexy! 'I was just coming to get you out of satsang,' she said. 'It's time for the Rolls-Royce darshan. Every day at this time the Bhagwan drives past in one of his Rolls-Royces.' Then she explained the point of the eighty Rolls-Royces. Not very convincingly. I still don't know what it was.

Seconds later this Rolls-Royce Silver Spur came crunching along Nirvana Drive with the Bhagwan himself at the wheel. There was quite a crowd and everyone except the ones with the video cameras bowed down and raised their hands in salute. 'Oooh,' squealed Modesty. 'Isn't he just the most beautiful, funny, happy person alive?' I thought he looked like an evil little bastard with his tubby figure and silver beard. I didn't care for his expression, nor for the way he fixed me with a stare. It was a bad moment. I didn't think he liked the look of me. But I didn't have too long to concentrate on the little man because as I stared at him I saw what I had come for. She was slight, and boyish, her mousey hair streaked blonde by the sun, but the face was the face in the photograph Jack had given me. Modesty saw me gazing. 'Her name is Ma Prem Vajra,' she said, giving her shoulder holster a hitch. 'Not your type.' I took the hint. Later that evening I saw her again but there was no way I could approach her inconspicuously. One of our group noticed me staring. He told me she worked in the greenhouse.

*   *   *

I was only allowed one day of indoor worship. Next day,
Tuesday, I had to go back to hard labour. I was getting
nervous. The helicopter was due in twenty-four hours. I
didn't see Cathy while I was out in the fields but that night
she came past with a group of girls fresh from swimming
in the lake. This time I was sure. I was on the point of
setting off after her and making some sort of contact when
my minder, Modesty, came up and sat next to me.

'You seem to have a bad case of the Ma Prem Vajras,'
she said icily. I wasn't sure if she was suspicious or just
jealous.

'Like you said. Not my type.' I smiled.

'You could have fooled me,' she said, dimpling. 'Ma
Prem Vajra is not for you. She's not happy here.'

That was interesting. 'Is she new?'

'No. She's been here as long as I have.'

'Which is how long?'

She closed her eyes. 'For ever,' she said.

Oh my God! Was I going to be glad to get out of this
place!

Wednesday was bad. I had another day in the fields and I
knew I wouldn't be finished until 6.30 p.m. That gave me
less than an hour to find Cathy, give her the pitch and get
her across three miles of rough country to the rendezvous
with the chopper. It couldn't be done. I tried to take the
afternoon off, appealed for another shot of the old satsang,
but our foreman wasn't having it. On our way home a
chopper flew over to the dried riverbed and sat hovering
over my kerosene 'J', then dipped and flew towards Portland. 'State Police,' said our foreman. 'Or maybe FBI.
They fly over all the time.' He switched on his CB radio.
'Security will have spotted him,' he said. 'But I'd better let
them know we're on the ball out here.'

Thursday was worse than the day before. It rained all

day and we were confined to barracks. I couldn't find Ma Prem Vajra, or Cathy, anywhere – not even in the greenhouse. Around seven I thought I heard a helicopter but it was raining too hard to be sure.

Friday was my last chance. I was cutting it awfully fine. At breakfast I told our group leader I was sick. He told me to report to the clinic. I could see he thought I was malingering. That was too bad. I had no option. The toilet was the only private place. I went in there and checked Cathy's photo just to be sure. Then I went over to the greenhouse. Cathy was there this time, potting plants with some other women. Even her gardening gloves were purple. There was no way I could approach discreetly, so I went outside feeling idiotic. Who should turn up but my friendly minder, the Modesty Blaise clone. She must have had sixth sense.

'I heard you were feeling sick,' she said. 'So I figured I'd find you here. Looking for healing herbs?'

'Just looking,' I said. 'I hear it's the biggest greenhouse in the State.'

'And you're the biggest ass-hole in the State,' she snarled. 'This is Rajneeshpuram not Club Med. You're here to love the Bhagwan and find yourself. Not to pick up chicks. You need more satsang.' And she walked me straight across to Satsang Central. You could hear them going 'Hoo! Hoo!' from 100 yards away. It was going to be another bad day.

I finally managed to escape around three o'clock and went straight back to the greenhouse, keeping a keen eye out for Modesty. As I neared the building half a dozen women came out. One was Cathy. I followed them over to the dining hall where they stopped. Then I got a break. The others went in and Cathy stayed out. She waved them goodbye and headed towards the A-frames. I pounced. We were in full view of the passers-by and there were plenty of them. But it was my only chance.

'Excuse me,' I said.

'You talking to me?' she asked.

'I think your name is Cathy,' I said.

There was no reaction. Just a blank stare. Either I was wrong or she was a good actress. I showed her the photograph. Just flashed it, then put it back in my pocket.

'Where in God's name did you get that?' So far, so good.

'Keep absolutely calm,' I said. 'Don't let anyone get suspicious. Act normal. I got the picture off your father. He sent me here with a letter. He thinks you want out.'

'Who *are* you?' She was very nervous and I couldn't blame her. 'I think you have been sent to test me!'

I didn't have much time. We were beginning to get funny looks. Any minute now Modesty and the goon squad would be along. I pulled out my picture – the one her father had written across. She glanced at it and seemed reassured. 'Very slowly now,' I said. 'Let's go and sit under that tree so we're away from the limelight.'

'This is crazy,' she said. But she was walking towards the tree.

'Act natural,' I repeated. 'We're just having a little chat about the meaning of meaning.'

We sat down under the tree and I gave her the letter from her old man. I just hoped that we didn't look too conspicuous. Men and women sometimes sit around under the trees reading Bhagwan tracts and talking garbage. We shouldn't have looked too out of place. Halfway through the first paragraph a tear started to trickle down her cheek. I was half pleased, half terrified. On the one hand it meant her father was right and she did want out; on the other it meant she was in danger of losing control.

'Get a grip on yourself, Cathy,' I said, 'and listen carefully. Your dad has sent me here to bring you home if you wish. If you're happy and don't want to leave, I will just walk away and go back where I came from.' I took the letter back. If there was to be any incriminating evidence

197

I wanted it to be found on me, not her.

'Nobody can leave here,' she said. 'I've tried twice. They have guns.'

'They pulled guns on you?'

'They told me they loved me and they sent me back. Now they watch me all the time. I'm scared.'

'Try to smile,' I said. 'Otherwise people will get suspicious.' I was smiling so much I had face-ache.

'We can't do it,' she said. 'There are too many of them.'

'No such word as "can't", Cathy,' I said. 'You know your dad. You know he wouldn't hire a man who couldn't do the job.'

She sighed; looked at me; gazed at the ground; looked back at me; almost smiled. 'I believe you,' she said. 'When can we go?'

'Right now,' I said.

She made to get up. 'I'll be right back when I've changed. And there are one or two people I want to say goodbye to.'

'I said, "Right now", Cathy. We've no time for any of that.'

She stared at me. I think she was beginning to realise I was serious. I stood up and held out a hand. 'We're walking out like a couple of lovebirds,' I said, 'holding hands and whispering into each other's shell-like ears. If we run into any of your friends, just nod. No chat. We're walking into the hills for some private mutual pleasure. They should know all about that here of all places.'

Her eyes narrowed. 'Just don't get any ideas,' she said. I liked that. It was a welcome touch of spirit. She took my hand and stood. 'Where are we going?'

'Ask no questions, hear no lies,' I replied. I didn't want to tell her about Jack's helicopter. If we were caught before we made the rendezvous, they'd make her talk. I wasn't about to take the risk.

It was deceptively easy at first. The worst we got were

funny looks. Just out of town there was a cluster of A-frames. We gave these a wide berth and struck up a narrow path through the juniper and sage-brush towards a rocky creek bed that lay in the hills. I was just beginning to relax when I heard an engine behind us. It sounded frantic. Menacing.

It was the goon squad pickup, going fast. A plume of dust spiralled out behind it. I grabbed Cathy by the shoulder and we hit the deck together and scrambled into the cover of a sage-brush. I manoeuvred into a position I could watch from, and saw the truck pull up outside one of the A-frames. A figure in maroon leapt out while another stayed in the cab and kept the engine running. Seconds later the maroon figure came running back and jumped in the cab. The pickup's engine revved, the gears slammed and it headed back towards town only to do a sudden U-turn and bump on to the open desert. It was heading straight for us.

I called out to Cathy to stay where she was and keep quiet. Meanwhile I scratched away some topsoil and buried the letter and photograph. They'd served their purpose. Without them we could at least pretend we'd come out for a quick roll in the sage-brush.

The truck came to a halt about fifty feet away and the two goons got out. One, naturally, was my friend Modesty, complete with Uzi and big Zeiss binoculars slung round her shapely neck. The other was the unpleasant Vietnam Vet swami who'd interviewed me the day I arrived. Modesty scanned the area with the glasses. 'I doubt they'd come this way,' she said. I could hear every word.

'Her friend said they'd come this way.' He was a real ape, this guy.

'Friends take care of friends,' said Modesty, crisply. 'We'll have to check out all Ma Prem Vajra's friends.'

'Should have checked out that Miller dude,' said Ape-man. 'I figured he was from the *National Enquirer* straight off.'

'I thought he was kinda cute,' said Modesty. 'Shows how wrong you can be. I guess they've gone some other way. We'd better get the road blocks alerted.' And they got back in the truck and headed off towards town again.

When I reached her Cathy was bundled in the foetal position, sobbing. 'It's OK,' I said. 'They're not coming back. Not for a while anyway.'

'I'm afraid,' she said, between sobs.

I pulled her to her feet. She needed the reassurance of physical contact. 'It's going to be all right,' I said, with a confidence I was far from feeling. 'John will look after you.'

She seemed to calm down a little. 'How far are we going?' she wanted to know.

'Not far,' I lied.

It was tough going. We had to keep below the skyline and duck down beneath the scrubby junipers; we had to listen like crazy for pursuit, for trucks, for footsteps, for choppers overhead, for those damn Dobermanns. I kept a tight hold of Cathy's hand so that I was almost pulling her along over the little hills and through the brush. She kept sobbing and asking how much further we had to go and did I know what I was doing and what the hell was I up to? Eventually we stopped for a quick breather and I told her a little more.

'A helicopter,' she said. 'And a British private eye. I'm surprised he didn't send a camera crew. I'm not going anywhere with you, you bastard.'

It was all the same to me. 'OK,' I said. 'So long. Nice knowing you. I have a helicopter to catch.' But there was no turning back now and she knew it as well as I did.

We kept going like this for the best part of three hours. She wasn't in great condition physically, so she was tired out. And she was emotionally very confused. I could hardly blame her for that. Luckily she was only little and it was no great sweat to drag her along with me. Eventually we reached the top of a ridge which I judged to be about ten minutes short of our destination. I paused and listened. No sound of pursuit. I snaked to the very summit and peered round a boulder. Good news and bad news! The good news was that the rendezvous was not more than ten minutes away. The bad news was that broadside on across the road, just where we wanted to cross it, there was a pickup truck. It didn't look like a Bhagwan truck – too beaten up. My guess was that it was an ambush mounted by the local rednecks. They were hoping to pump some lead into swamis.

I told Cathy. Our chopper was due an hour before sunset. The sun was getting dangerously low. We were going to have to chance it. 'Those damn rednecks,' said Cathy. She may have wanted out but she still had a lot of Bhagwan loyalty to shed.

'We'll cross higher up,' I said, and we set off again, keeping below the crest of the ridge. After a couple of hundred yards I made Cathy freeze. A vehicle was coming from the ranch. It was travelling fast. He must have seen the pickup as he came over the head of the pass because there was a squeal of brakes, then a crash of gears, followed almost at once by a shotgun blast. Then another. 'Move it!' I snarled at Cathy.

'They're shooting down there!' Cathy was in a blue funk. She was frozen with fright. I yanked at her. Hard. In response to the shotgun fire there was a twenty-round crackle of automatic fire. It sounded like an Uzi.

'They'll be too busy with each other to bother with us,' I said. 'So shift your ass.'

She did as she was told. As we crossed the crest we could see two vehicles. One of the blue Bhagwan trucks was stopped dead, its windshield stove in and fragmented like a spider's web. As we watched, a rifle shot rang out and one of the blue pickup's tyres went flat. It was a regular old gunfight. We jigged from boulder to boulder and bush to bush, always trying to keep something between us and the source of the gunfire. At the bottom of the slope we paused behind a clump of sage-brush. 'On your marks,' I whispered. 'Now get set . . . *go!*'

Halfway across the road there was a familiar little ping I hadn't heard in ages. A small explosion of dirt erupted just in front of us. Seconds later I heard the rifle. Not a very near miss, but close enough. Those bastard rednecks had spotted our magenta. We covered the second half of the road in record time and dived headlong into the sage-brush on the other side. As we lay there panting, I heard the sound of more vehicles proceeding fast from Rajneeshpuram. The ambushed goons had obviously radioed for help. Round the bend in the road came three blue Bhagwan trucks, crammed with armed swamis in burgundy. I smiled. It looked as if everyone had plenty to be getting on with. No need for them to worry with us.

'We were lucky,' I told Cathy. She nodded. 'Now, listen . . .' I explained exactly where the chopper was coming in and what we would have to do.

'OK, OK,' she kept saying. 'Let's do it. I don't need to know all this. Just let's do it.'

'I'm telling you,' I said, 'in case I can't make it and you have to do it on your own.'

There was a long pause. 'Oh, sorry,' she said. She looked dangerously close to tears again. 'I don't even know your name,' she said.

'That's the least of your problems,' I said. And we set off. There was plenty of gunfire at first. Then nothing. I didn't like that.

We almost blew it at the lip of the canyon. When we reached it I saw two rednecks crouching behind a boulder covering the road with a rifle and a shotgun. The sides of the canyon were slippery with scree. One false move would have sent a pebble or something rattling down towards the rednecks and we'd have been dead in a flash. They meant business. We should have made a detour but we had no time. We had to take the shortest route and that meant getting down the canyon wall and crossing behind the rednecks. We just had to go softly, softly and pray. Not only pray that the rednecks didn't see us, but also that we weren't spotted by those three truckloads of avenging swamis.

We did well. Baden-Powell would have been proud of us. Likewise my old mates in the regiment. We were halfway there when there was another engine sound. This time from above. We still had quarter of a mile to go. 'Go for it, Cathy,' I said. 'If they do see us they'll be too freaked out by the chopper.' I hoped I was right. Every step we took set off a fresh avalanche of pebbles. But the chopper's engines cut out everything else. He was right overhead. We had to hurry or we'd miss him. Then suddenly there was no more slope and we were out on our little landing ground. Only a few yards to the burnt out 'J'. One thing about a job like this; there's never time to relax.

As we reached the 'J' I glanced up. On the other side of the clearing was a handful of armed swamis. They were running towards us. And the chopper wasn't even down yet. As it came in the swamis stopped and began to gesticulate. Thank God, I thought. Maybe they think it's one of theirs. It was almost down. The noise was deafening. The blades were whipping up dust and flattening the grass. Christ, I thought. Maybe it *was* one of the Bhagwan's choppers. We'd look pretty silly climbing on to one of the enemy's whirlybirds. But there was no point in even thinking about that.

The pilot swung the machine into the wind and set it down with a couple of bumps. Cathy started to run round the tail to get at the door and I had to rugby tackle her to stop her getting mashed up by the tail rotors. The Rajneeshis had realised it wasn't one of theirs now. There was no seagull logo on the cockpit. They were charging across the grass. One or two had stopped and were raising their Uzis. The door of the chopper swung open. I threw Cathy in and piled in after her. The first of the oncoming swamis was only a few feet away. At the controls was a short guy with a great beer belly bursting out of a Grateful Dead T-shirt. He was grinning like a maniac and gave me a thumbs-up. I gave him one back and shouted 'Take her up! Take her up!' He couldn't have heard me but he took her up anyway. I don't think any of the swamis fired. They were so close they couldn't have missed. Bye bye, Bhagwan!

It's always a bit of an anti-climax when the job's over. It's a little like sex. Or a game of polo. We were met at Portland. A big stretched limo was waiting outside the chain-link fence. Cathy and her aunt travelled in the back. I sat up front with the driver, feeling like the hired help. They dropped me off at the Hilton. I thought they might at least lower the plate-glass window so I could say goodbye, but nothing happened so I shuffled off in the direction of a shower, a stiff drink and a large steak. Jack was as good as his word. I got a cheque a day or so later. I never did hear from the Bhagwan, though.

Up to Date

I suppose many people think of me as some kind of bodysnatcher, but I have only spirited people away when I've considered that I was helping to enforce the law or natural justice by grabbing someone out of their usual or unusual surroundings.

One born-again Christian mother in Tennessee sent me off to Guatemala to search for her bible-thumping son who had gone there to do missionary work and had vanished. She wanted him home, if he was still alive. He was. He had given up religion, dropped out, discovered native women and didn't want to come home, so I just left him there. A shadowy organisation in New York hired me to get down to Paraguay to check out for their own peace of mind the reports that Dr Josef Mengele, the Auschwitz camp doctor, was really dead. He was. I left him there too!

There has to be some fairly compelling moral reason for me to undertake this kind of assignment. That's why I've walked away from lucrative offers, like the wealthy Iranian family who wanted me to smuggle their uncle out of the Ayatollah's Tehran to their new château just outside Paris. The old boy's signature was needed on the Swiss bank account to let them get their hands on the dough they had amassed in shady deals with the Shah's sister Princess Ashraf before the mullahs took over. Sure, I've got sympathy for anybody living in Iran under Khomeini, but I wasn't about to risk my neck or any of my team just to let them enjoy their ill-gotten gains. I turned down £250,000 on that job.

When the luscious Jerry Hall, Mick Jagger's lady, was in Barbados facing some time in a stinking Caribbean jail, I was invited to meet a wealthy Jagger sympathiser in Claridge's in Mayfair to discuss snatching Jerry away from under the noses of the island cops and back to California where a good LA lawyer could probably have kept her safe from extradition. I don't know if the guy thought he was doing Jerry and Mick a favour, but I wanted to wait and see if justice would take its course. At the end of the day Jerry was cleared of the dope smuggling allegations, although if she had been jailed on a trumped-up charge, I would have asked for another meeting with Mick's friend to discuss the project a little further.

Most of my life since the Army has been spent around music and showbiz. I suppose it's the legacy of those nights at the Majestic Ballroom in Motherwell when we used to get dressed up in those outrageous suits and were stage-struck by stars like Screaming Lord Sutch. Luckily the guys in that sort of world always need people like me. The Army teaches you discipline and organisation and how to look after yourself if you're threatened. These things are in short supply among rock stars and entertainers but they are very much in demand. So, on the whole, I have always been able to earn a living in a world I love and among people I like.

I'm addicted to showbusiness. I don't mean *everything* to do with the entertainment industry, let alone *everyone*. Some of the most pathetic individuals I've ever met have been famous actors or musicians. But there is an attitude among showbusiness folk which you don't get elsewhere. They're really prepared to go out and enjoy themselves. And they don't care what the rest of the world thinks. I admire that and I can identify with it.

Take my friend Oliver Reed. We were having a drink in

206

his hotel in Los Angeles one night – me and my wife Sarah, Ollie and his then girlfriend Josephine, now Mrs Reed. He was in town for the making of the movie *Sting Two*. At one point Sarah remarked on the eagle's head tattoo on his shoulder. 'Yes,' he said. 'That's Dickinton Bird. He perches on my cock.'

It was just Ollie's idea of a joke, but he decided on the spot that it should be more than just an innocent fib as a conversation piece. He turned to me and asked where he could find a tattooist. I advised him against it. I have two tattoos from my army days. I wish I hadn't. But once Oliver gets hold of an idea, he won't let go. 'I want Dickinton Bird's talons tattooed on my cock,' he insisted. So we left the girls and headed off in a hired limo.

The first stop was a tattoo parlour on Sunset Boulevard, opposite the Hyatt Hotel. The proprietor there wasn't pleased when Oliver pulled out his willie. He called Oliver a faggot, there was a brief fracas and we drove off. I thought it was all over then and we could go home. No such luck. Unfortunately Ollie's driver said he knew a place a few blocks away on Hollywood Boulevard. This one was run by a Chinaman. The Chinaman was more polite than the previous tattooist, but he also declined the job. However there was a young Chinese girl there and she said she would do it for him. And she did. It looked horribly painful and I was so impressed that despite all my good resolutions to the contrary, I allowed myself to be tattooed again. Mine was a discreet shoulder job saying simply 'Oliver. 1981.'

On our way back, Oliver swore me to total secrecy. He didn't want anyone to get a hold of it, as it were. Minutes later we were passing that well-known British expatriate watering-hole, the Cock and Bull on Sunset Boulevard, and Oliver ordered the driver to pull over. We were hardly inside the door when Oliver had his flies open and was displaying Dickinton Bird's new perch to anyone who was interested and even to a few who didn't have the slightest interest.

Ollie had his ornithological rarity out again two nights later at a Hollywood party. He whipped it out for the benefit of an elderly lady who seemed mildly surprised until an old gentleman came over and said, very politely, to him: 'Sir, would you kindly stop waving that insignificant thing at my wife.' Then he took his wife by the elbow and walked off with her.

My career in music started in 1975 when I met Alex Harvey at the Reading Festival. I was backstage. I was still in the Army and I met a bloke who said the organisers were looking for people to help with security. So I went along and at one moment Alex's manager tried to get up on stage. He was a big fat lump and at the time I didn't know who he was. He was swearing and cursing and making unprintable remarks about my ancestry and I was trying to throw him off because he didn't have a pass. Afterwards he invited me for a drink in the bus to say sorry because I had just been doing my job.

Alex was there in the hospitality tent with the rest of the Sensational Alex Harvey Band. Later when I left the Army for the second time, Alex was on tour with the Who. It was a big round-Britain tour called 'The Who put the Boot in.' They did Cardiff Castle, Parkhead in Glasgow, Charlton Athletic's football ground. Big venues. There was the Who, Alex and Little Feat and the Outlaws. We got on so well together that I continued to work with him regularly from then until he died in 1982.

I started doing security and ended as his tour manager. The security job was a bit of a joke because he wasn't really big enough to warrant security and all it really involved was getting drunk with him every night. He was a very bizarre, rather wonderful man. They say he was a punk before his time and I think maybe that's right.

I remember on an American tour reporters would

always ask, 'Who was the biggest influence on your musical career?' It's a stock question for music hacks and the guy who's being interviewed always thinks for a moment and then he says, 'Elvis Presley', or maybe, 'Chuck Berry'. Well, they did in those days. So the very first time Alex was asked the question, he thought for a moment and said: 'My Auntie Jessie. She was a three-fingered blues guitarist. She lost the other fingers working underground for the French Resistance in the war.'

The American press loved it. 'What was your first job before you were a rock star?'

'I was an apprentice lion-tamer with Bertram Mills' Circus.' Another time he'd say he had been a trainee frogman, or a cabin boy propositioned by a sixteen-stone gay stoker. Every interview he gave he produced a different set of stories. They were all printed so he created a whole set of characters: one for Memphis, another for Austin, a third for Albuquerque. And so on all round the States.

He always did have outrageous ideas. He used to do that old Fred Astaire number 'Dancing Cheek to Cheek', and he had three backing singers. They were rather sophisticated girls in long evening gowns and when it got to the 'Cheek to Cheek' bit, they'd suddenly twirl round and present their backsides to the audience: there was no back to the lower part of their dresses. Just bare bums.

When I ran the Vortex in Soho, Alex was on the permanent guest list. But invariably when he turned up I would get the same message from the bouncer on the door. 'Alex Harvey's here.'

'Well, let him in.'

'He won't come in. He wants you to search him.'

So I'd have to go down to the door and Alex would tell me that he had a blade hidden about his person and he bet I couldn't find it. Well, Alex was quite clever about that sort of thing but then so were the I R A and as I had been on the search team in Ulster it was really no contest. I always searched him out of courtesy, found the blade and let him in. But it became a sort of vendetta. Alex was determined that he was going to get into the club carrying a weapon. Every night we went through the same routine. Every night I got the call. Every night I searched him. And every night I found the blade. He would have gone on playing that game for ever.

I remember one night Alex turned up at the club at 11 p.m. on a Monday night and said he was going to play. He had with him an American bagpiper, also drunk. My stage manager already had his work cut out but Alex was a friend so I said he and his pal could do their number immediately before the headline act. He and his mate went on and Alex sang twelve verses of a Scottish dirge so obscure that even Andy Stewart wouldn't have heard of it. I don't know who was more confused – me, Alex, the American bagpiper or the punks!

Once in Liverpool, after the big band had broken up, Alex hadn't a lot of money and he was drinking heavily. I had a great idea. His big hit had been 'Delilah' and he always wore those distinctive black and white striped T-shirts. So I said, 'Why don't you get one of those inflatable dolls from a sex shop and dress it in a black and white T-shirt? Then you can go on stage and play with it while you're singing Delilah.'

It wasn't such a clever idea after all. We had a terrible time trying to find a sex shop. Then there was a scene in the shop with the proprietor refusing to believe I wanted the doll for a stage set. Naturally Alex took the proprietor's side and kept calling me a dirty pervert and trying to get me to buy the de luxe model with all the optional extras. Alex dressed it in black stockings, suspender belt and a T-shirt and took it down to breakfast in our hotel dining room where he proceeded to feed it on porridge which dribbled all down its front. The waitresses refused to serve them any more. And when he took it on stage that night he attacked it with a knife. By the end of the tour the doll was patched up with gaffer tape from head to toe.

He was very much ahead of his time, Alex. Other bands used to watch and copy – notably the Tubes, and David Bowie hung around Alex a lot. He was a great influence on me personally, just watching the way he dealt with people. He died much too young. It was a heart attack driving back from a concert in Belgium. Undoubtedly it was the drinking that had brought it on. He was a typical Glaswegian in that way – all booze but no drugs. And he'd been in Rock 'n' Roll for ever. When I watched that brilliant TV series *Tutti Frutti* with a terrible rock band called the Majestics, it was just like being back with Alex all over again.

He was always playing games. He used to say to me that he was going to escape from me before the show started and if he got away he wouldn't go on stage. So I used to spend a lot of my time literally handcuffed to him. It was really quite serious. I was afraid he really would get away and not turn up on stage. A non-appearance could have finally finished his career. Promoters won't back a performer who develops a reputation for unreliability, no matter how big they are.

Alex was my first real introduction to music but I came back to it again when I moved to California after the Biggs snatch in 1981. I'd gone to hand over some photos of the snatch to a picture agency and decided to stay on. I met a friend of a friend who was opening a country and western bar just south of Ventura, outside Los Angeles, so I ran that for a while. Then I met another friend of a friend who ran a Swiss heavy metal band called Krokus. I kid you not, there's more to Swiss music than yodelling and melodic cuckoo clocks. I went to Germany with them for a show and everyone was there – Ozzy Osbourne, Michael

Schenker, Def Leppard, Iron Maiden – the lot! One of the people I met was Chris Glen, the bass player with Michael Schenker. He'd originally been the bass player with, guess who, Alex Harvey. And he asked if I'd travel with Michael Schenker to Japan as tour manager.

It's just simple logistics, being a tour manager. If you've been in the Army and learned to take a platoon out on an exercise, then you can take a band on tour. It's making sure things happen – being the co-ordinator between the management and the record company and the band. The management books the tour; the travel agent books the hotels and the flights; the promoter books the shows. You just go with the band, make sure they get from A to B, collect the money, pay wages, hotel bills and generally manage the band while they're on tour. You need no knowledge of music whatever. You just need a sound sense of logistics and a little book-keeping ability. Sometimes you're carrying around twenty or thirty thousand dollars. There's a lot of self-discipline involved. You're in charge. There's no way you can go out and get pissed till three in the morning. You've got the responsibility for the smooth running of the tour and sometimes for the sanity and safety of your stars. And that can be a knife-edge job if you have to cope with rock stars who are downright loonies.

When I took Schenker to Japan I knew by his reputation that Michael was a bit of an eccentric. He's a German, and a stereotype of your young Aryan he-man, blond-haired blue-eyed bursting with energy and vigour. But he's also almost totally devoid of discipline and, like a lot of rock stars, tends to overdo the drink a wee bit.

Michael, who was the founder of the heavy metal band UFO, is one of those musicians who is not particularly big in the US but is a megastar in Japan. And he has a temper to match. The tour didn't get off to a brilliant start when we set up to play a stadium in Hiroshima. I was running through a sound rehearsal, including special effects when we went to check the wiring for a pyrotechnic display where Michael would come on stage as 'Captain Nemo', introduced by a spectacular ear-splitting explosion, a fireball and clouds shooting up into the air. The Japanese stadium manager listened patiently to what I had in mind. Then he shook his head. 'You no make bang,' he announced.

I explained to him, 'Don't worry, there's no danger. It's just a blinding light and a lot of noise. No damage. No one gets hurt.'

He shook his head. 'You no make bang.'

I went through it again, adding, 'We have a fire crew standing by, first-aid medics. The crowd will love it. It is part of our act. It is an important part of our display.' The Japanese wouldn't be budged.

I was exasperated. 'You are cheating the audience of a great spectacle. Why are you doing this?'

He shrugged. 'Audience not like this display anyway.'

'Oh, you're Mister Knowall. You know in advance what the fans are gonna like and what they're not gonna like?'

He smiled serenely. 'Mister Millah. This Hiroshima. People not want flash, bang and cloud over city.' I suppose he had a point.

Michael Schenker came on stage as Captain Nemo to a drum roll and a few strobe lights. It wasn't quite the same. I don't know if that's what upset him but after the show, in the early hours of the morning, a roadie knocked on my door and said, 'John, I think you'd better do something about Michael, he's smashing up his room.' I bounded to the elevator and zoomed up to Michael's suite on the top floor. From the corridor I could hear the sound of furniture being taken apart. I hammered on the door.

'Fuck off,' Michael screamed at me.

'Let me in, you crazy bastard!'

The door stayed firmly locked. I was listening to the noise of the suite being smashed to pieces so I thought it wasn't going to add much to the wreckage if I kicked down the door. I did. Michael was pleased to see me. He was trying to throw a heavy table lamp with just one hand. His other hand was busy holding the phone to his ear. He wanted both hands free to inflict maximum damage so he handed the phone to me and growled in his best guttural German accent, 'Speak to this Jewish bastard! Damned accountants, money-lenders, idiots, that's all his race are good for.'

I grabbed the phone. 'Hello?' On the other end of the line, in Los Angeles, was manager David Krebs. Now David has managed bands like AC/DC and Aerosmith, so he was used to tantrums and long-distance abuse by telephone.

'John,' he said calmly. 'Michael seems a little bit upset. It might bring him back down to earth if you take him downtown to pay a visit to the atom bomb site.'

'Huh? David, I'm *in* a bloody bomb site.' Michael, with both hands now free, was crashing a glass coffee table into a display cabinet and beheading delicate little Japanese statues.

'What makes you think a visit to the atom bomb memorial is going to do the slightest thing to cool his anger against Jewish people in general, and you in particular?' I asked Krebs.

David was smooth and unctuous. 'Give him a few minutes quiet contemplation about the atom bomb.'

'You want this maniac to meditate about the Bomb?'

'Precisely, John,' he replied soothingly. And his voice hardened and he added, 'then you kick his ass and remind him of the ethnic origins of Albert Einstein!' Michael never went to the bomb site, but he did behave himself a little better after I relayed David's message.

The rest of the tour went smoothly, except for the minor

214

interruption of Chris Glen being 'arrested' in Tokyo. We had both gone out after a show to have a serious drink in Shinjuku, one of the seedier parts of the city, when Chris was pounced on by a Japanese groupie as we entered a bar. She was a heavy metal freak. Ripped stockings, short skirt, dodgy hairdo, funny legs, studded belt, handcuff dangling from one skinny wrist, the whole bit.

'You Cliss Glen?' she squealed.

'Sure am,' Chris replied modestly.

I interrupted. 'Chris, stop messin' about. Let's hit the bar for a bloody drink.' But he was doing his swanky star act, letting the girl fuss over him, wasting valuable drinking time. I lost my patience. 'Oh, you want to spend the night chatting her up? Well now you've definitely got her all to yourself.' I grabbed the spare loop of handcuff and whacked it on Chris's wrist. Then I stormed off to the bar and started doing something urgent about my powerful thirst.

I caught a couple of glimpses of Chris and the girl as the night wore on. He was getting distinctly uncomfortable not being able to shake off the groupie who was beginning to get a bit too frisky for comfort. Worse still every time he needed a piss he had to drag her into the gents with him, and she had him off into the ladies a couple of times. That'll teach him, I thought.

At the end of the night, Chris came over to me uncomfortably, with the half-pissed groupie in tow. 'John, I want to introduce you to Miki,' he said.

'I don't really want to know, Chris.'

'You'd never guess where she's from, John.'

'Shepherd's Bush, I suppose. Listen, Chris I'm not interested where the hell she's from.'

'You might like to know she's from Sapporo, John.'

'So what?'

'That's about five hundred miles away on another Japanese island.'

'So, she's a country girl from out of town.'

'And the keys to these handcuffs are in the drawer of her dressing table. That's also in Sapporo.' He raised his arm with the drunken groupie hanging limply from his wrist. 'You're the tour manager. You caused the problem. Now you get me free.'

I piled them both into the back of a cab and took them back to our hotel where I summoned the maintenance man to the room. He had a bag of hammers, chisels, hacksaws, but he took one look at the handcuffs and shook his head. 'I cannot cut these,' he decided.

'For God's sake, why not?'

Chris and the girl were sprawled out on the bed, both nodding off to sleep. The maintenance man pointed to some Japanese characters on the handcuffs. 'Police issue,' he announced. 'No touch, no damage.'

It took me another twenty minutes to give Chris and the girl a thorough body search, looking for any illicit substances which might accidentally have fallen into pockets or purses. Then I was confident enough to take them to the local police station.

'Good evening, officers. My friend and I are visiting from England and we have caught this young woman with some stolen police handcuffs. As you can see, my friend has arrested her. If you'll just unlock these cuffs we can be about our business and this woman will be your prisoner.' Warily, they fetched a set of keys and Chris was finally unlocked from the groupie who'd passed out dead drunk. I didn't wait to make any more excuses. I steered Chris out of the police station and shouted over my shoulder: 'Be careful, she's from Sapporo, she might be dangerous.' The cops just looked inscrutable.

Some music stars are fun to be around. Others aren't. They're just plain boring. The variety's great. Different city every night, different stadium, different hotel. Even the dressing rooms are different and the objectives are different. But apart from Alex, I've never been really close to any of them. I suppose it's because nearly all of them have only one topic of conversation and that's music, about which I know and really care very little. There are exceptions but by and large it's music, music and more music. And I'm afraid, too, that with one or two exceptions, they're no brighter than your average private soldier in the Army, so you're often having to clear up their daft mistakes. The other day, for instance, I was in the States with a band who had better be nameless. We were due to go over the frontier to play a gig in Canada and had sent the heavy luggage on ahead. And what do two of the band do? You've guessed it. They packed their passports. So I have to get on a plane, fly to Calgary, get their passports out of their cases and fly back to the States again so they can get over the border.

One big star who turned out disappointingly to be an insecure pain in the arse was Lou Reed. His manager Eric Kronfeld offered me the job of touring in Europe with Lou. That sort of nannying gets boring after a while but it pays the bills. So I took the assignment. It was one of the least memorable experiences of my life. Lou is a big cult figure in Europe and he was pulling in capacity audiences of up to 70,000 people at venues in Spain.

Before some of the gigs we'd do 'in-store' promotions where he was expected to go to some big department store, preen himself in the record department and sign some autographs. He was besieged by adoring young fans, some of whom had brought along their entire album collections, including classics from his old Velvet Underground days and the Andy Warhol-designed *Banana* album, expecting their hero to sign them. Lou would get bored and say, 'That's it, I'm only signing one more.' Then he would flounce out and go back to his hotel. I hated to see

217

the disappointment on the fans' faces. That's no way for a performer to treat his customers.

And he had a couple of blind spots, literally. Without his glasses, he was almost as blind as a bat. One night before we went on stage in a bullring in Spain, before a crowd of about 70,000, Lou summoned me back stage. I thought it was going to be another trivial complaint or moaning session. All he said was, 'John, I can't quite see what's going on but I think these audiences are throwing things at the stage. You've got to stop them.'

With such a capacity crowd I didn't know there was much I could do, but I did place extra security down below the front of the stage. The Spanish crowd were good-natured and no trouble at all. I couldn't see any missiles being aimed in our direction. Until Lou was egged on the druggie number 'Heroin'. Then they came flying through the darkness, disposable hypodermic syringes, dozens of them, landing in front of the stage, just outside Lou's blurred field of vision. It was like a shower of darts with someone hoping to score 'One hundred and eighty' by landing a bull's-eye on Lou. I don't know, they might have been AIDS-infected. Or they might just have been trying to prick the prick's ego.

Ian Asprey of the Cult, now he's different – a fun guy, but a bit weird. I can talk army with Ian. He's heavily into militaria. He's an expert on the strategy and history of the Vietnam War and he owns thousands of pounds worth of authentic uniforms. Unfortunately most of them are the genuine Nazi item. The first time I saw him dressed up was at a Billy Idol concert and Ian rolled in backstage on a skateboard, dressed in a Hitler Youth outfit.

On one US tour we went to a blues club in Washington DC for a little late-night entertainment. When I say blues, I mean the clientele was almost entirely black. Ian turned up for our night out dressed up as Adolf Hitler. We got past the door OK because I had VIP passes, but I had to tuck him in a darkened corner once inside the club. However, he got fidgety and wanted to go on stage.

That great black blues singer Coco Taylor was the star of the evening but she graciously agreed to let Ian on stage after her second set. I warned him, 'This is a black club and I don't think black people generally are Hitler's greatest fans.' He was unapologetic and emerged from the shadows into the spotlight on stage, lurching up to the mike in the whole Nazi regalia. There was uproar and outrage. I jumped up and explained, 'We're making a movie in town and Ian is playing a spoof Nazi nutcase. We've come straight from the film set. Please give us a break.' I grabbed the high-peaked cap from him, made him open the tunic down to the waist and pulled his trousers over the glistening jackboots. We got out alive at the end of a very nervous night for me.

But Ian is one of the few people who can lead me astray. I'm not normally given to acts of vandalism to let off steam. But to my shame I joined in enthusiastically with Ian one night at a resort called Lake Geneva in Wisconsin. We had become restless with the clockwork-smooth boredom of our hotel so we sneaked on to the golf course one night to cause a bit of mayhem. The course had been designed by Jack Nicklaus and was beautifully laid out with one of those white two-bar fences running all round it. I've always wanted to smash a vehicle through one of those fences, just like you see on the movies.

Ian egged me on and we stole a golf cart and tore round the greens at about 10 m.p.h. smashing through the fence with every turn. Hotel security turned out to capture us and we ended up hiding in a bunker with the golf cart camouflaged behind some bushes near us. There were too many criss-cross tyre tracks for the security men to get a lead on our position. So they gave up. At least we thought they had. They went off into the darkness, and as Ian and I crept back towards the hotel, we found the executive private airstrip at the edge of the golf course. Now you're talking! We clambered into one of the light aircraft and Ian said, 'Pity we can't start it up and buzz the hotel.'

No, we didn't take off on a kamikaze mission. But I've been in aircraft often enough to know that if you hit the right switches, you can get the engine running. So I flicked a few buttons and the propellor started to turn over. That's when the cops arrived. They took us back to the hotel and threatened to throw out the entire touring crew and band, about twenty people. Ian and I had our tails between our legs and we did a deal. We woke the tour bus driver and he drove the bus to a parking lot outside the hotel grounds and Ian and I had to spend the night sleeping in the unheated bus. We shivered all night. We could see the lights of the hotel, Swiss, efficient, warm and cosy. And we had to pay a small fortune in damages next morning for repairs to the golf greens and the fence.

It's not the first time my star chums and I have ended up with egg on our faces. I remember one incident in New York when we were down on the docks beside the Hudson River at 4 a.m., shooting scenes for Billy Idol's video 'Hot in the City'.

There was a break in filming and we were all cheered up by the sight of this gorgeous blonde who turned up at the chain link fence beside the waterfront and began a slow, erotic strip. We watched, mouths watering, as she took off her blouse, wafted it gently in the air and ever so slowly began to twirl round and unhook her bra. The coffee break was over but nobody was getting back to work. We were using a whole bunch of Harley Davidson motor bikes on the video and we drew them round in a semi-circle with the headlights beamed in on the blonde who was by now waving a shapely leg and peeling away a stocking from a black suspender belt. There was a general groan of mounting sexual excitement and a great cheer began echoing round the docks. It was too much for Billy. The mystery stripper was obviously there for his benefit, he thought, since he was the big sex symbol. He tugged my sleeve and whispered out of the corner of his mouth, 'Get over there and get her phone number, quick!' I was about to detach myself from the rest of the audience when the stripper turned her back towards us and bent over, leather miniskirt riding up over her hips. And then we all saw the bulge of testicles and willie squeezing out of the gusset of the brief knickers.

There was an embarrassed general return to work with red-faced randy production crews all lying and saying to each other, 'Well, of course, I knew all along it was a guy. Never fooled me. Spotted it a mile away.' All except one of the lighting men who hadn't been paying much attention when we all thought it was a nymphomaniac girl. As soon as he realised it was a transvestite pervert he sneaked up to the blonde and passed a note when he thought no one else was looking.

In 1981 I went to Jamaica for the first time. It was the Jamaican World Music Festival and it was a big deal – the Beach Boys, Aretha Franklin – all sorts. It made a lot of money but the problem with Jamaica was that you couldn't take the money out. Some of the American backers of the festival were left with a whole lot of surplus Jamaican funds, and they decided the only thing they could do was to invest in a nice place in Jamaica.

Politically Jamaica has had a peculiar time. First there was a long period under Prime Minister Michael Manley who makes Neil Kinnock look like Maggie Thatcher. Then they elected Edward Seaga who makes Maggie Thatcher look like Neil Kinnock. Talk about opposites! Seaga was ... is ... a thorough-going capitalist. Apparently one of my friends involved in the 1981 Music Festival had got the impression that Seaga's government was considering allowing gambling on the island to boost the tourist business. Manley naturally disapproved of such a thing. So this friend and his associates decided to start a glossy, glitzy casino, and the place they settled on was Fairfield, just outside Montego Bay.

Fairfield used to be the best country club in the whole Caribbean. Hoad and Laver played on the grass tennis court; there was a racetrack and a championship golf course. The Great House, which is what they call stately homes out there, had an Olympic pool. It also had a 200-seat theatre, cocktail bar, five-star restaurant and half a dozen very lavish suites. There were sixty acres of grounds with cottages. Quite some place.

The theatre was run by a local amateur dramatics group and there was a small private hospital in the grounds. Because no one had been paying it much attention, the foliage had encroached more than somewhat. The hard core was intact but it needed a lick of paint and a trim round the edges of the hedges. The grass was six-foot high. In other words, the place was a wee bit run down. Naturally, my friend asked if I would come out and do the job. I was under the impression that the casino licence was imminent and there was no time to waste. But you can never be too sure of anything in Jamaica. Nothing about Jamaica or Jamaicans is ever what it seems.

Apart from putting the white lines back on the tennis court and scything down the elephant grass, I was also having to do a certain amount of wheeling and dealing. I initially assumed that my friend and his associates owned Fairfield but it wasn't as simple as that. At one point the place had been owned by a syndicate of doctors, who then passed it on to another medical man who wanted to turn Fairfield into a snake venom clinic. The snake doctor failed to get the necessary permits for this and sold on to my man, the American rock promoter. Now, however, a previous partner in the doctors' practice, a powerful politician, was claiming that he was still owed a lot of money from the property transfer deals. He wanted his money, and since the new owner was not around in person, the one getting hassled was yours truly.

The original deal had been for a week or two, but it was beginning to stretch, so I phoned my wife Sarah and she and our baby daughter flew out from England to join me. We were living in our own house in our own coconut grove about two hundred yards from the Great House. In the garden we grew mango, pawpaw, banana, plantain – which is similar to banana but can be cooked – tangerine, avocado, pear, lime, lemon, breadfruit, sarasap and coconut. In the house we had Sadie who was nanny and housekeeper and all-round treasure.

My brief was to infiltrate the local establishment. I was supposed to make a lot of friends at the highest level so we'd have well-placed allies when the time came to dish out gambling licenses to reputable international applicants. Money was no object and I was to get alongside all the local policymakers I could fit in my pocket. So, swallowing hard, I bought a Porsche, a jeep, a string of polo ponies, and Sarah and I started to give parties. It was paradise but we worked extremely hard. Fairfield was beginning to look like it had done in the old days, that is, brilliant. That sort of renaissance doesn't just happen. It must have taken me half an hour each morning to give out the orders to the ever-increasing army of gardeners, builders, decorators and all-purpose dogsbodies I was taking on.

We had credit wherever we went and the money from the States came flooding into the local bank with stunning regularity. The manager and I were drinking companions. And so were local politicians who I cultivated as bosom buddies.

But there's always a price to pay in return for favours. One request came from a guy I took an instant liking to.

He was smart, and very ambitious and as straight as a politician can be. One day not long after I'd first met him, he asked if I could help him tape record a conversation with someone who was coming to pay him a visit. I'd given him a lot of bullshit about security operations, so he guessed I could help. I lent him one of my miniature tape-recorders – about four inches by two. It was nothing tremendously sophisticated, but it would do the job. He put it in his top pocket, bugged the conversation and seemed well pleased.

A while later he asked if I could plant a telephone bug inside someone's office. 'No problem,' I said. 'But whose office?' He mentioned an address way down south, in the capital, Kingston. This did set a few alarm bells ringing. It was the office of a very high-ranking political figure who could make life very uncomfortable for me if I stepped out of line with him. I had met him twice – at a reception in Kingston and a party in Montego Bay. I hadn't liked what I'd seen. I'm no great judge of character but he struck me as combining low animal cunning and arrogance in equal quantities. It wasn't an appealing mix and most people who knew him seemed to share my views.

The buzz was that he was not someone who would let moral scruples get in his way. But my new-found ally in Montego Bay was going for broke. He didn't like the big cheese in Kingston, and he could see him, among other things, as a political rival and an obstacle to his own progress. So he wanted him out of the way. The best way of doing that, he reckoned, was to bug his office when he was working in the hope of getting some dirt on him.

I liked my local buddy. I didn't like the other guy. I was socialising too much. I was just a touch bored with the lotus life. I thought this sounded like a bit of a challenge and a bit of fun. It was silly of me, but, what the hell! 'O K,' I agreed. 'I'll bug his office.'

I told him what I needed and he picked it up in Miami on

his next trip to the States. As a government man himself, he enjoyed diplomatic immunity which was a big advantage. It meant you could ease in and out with God knows what in your luggage. You never got searched. You never had to listen to those five dire words – 'Have you anything to declare?'

As soon as I'd got the gear I went down to Kingston to set the thing up. As you may have realised by now I'm a great believer in the old army adage about 'Bullshit baffles Brains'. Jamaica was all bullshit and no brains. If they weren't high on ganja they were zonked on rum. It was therefore no problem whatever to gain access to the office I wanted to monitor.

Once there, a few judiciously dropped names and winning smiles were enough to charm the secretary and enabled me to establish that her boss was out for a long, largely liquid, lunch. After a while she went off, for whatever she wanted, leaving me with the office to myself. It took me only two or three minutes to slip five hundred dollars worth of voice-activated radio transmitter into the telephone. When the secretary came back I was still immersed in the sports pages of the *Daily Gleaner*. A few minutes later I looked at my watch, said I couldn't wait any longer and would ring her boss at home some other time. She just grunted and away I went.

An English friend who just happened to be visiting was waiting outside in a hire car. Together we found a safe place where we could hook a receiver up to a small tape-recorder, with a ninety-minute tape in place. The idea was to put in fresh tapes every day. I never even bothered to listen to the results. The patois was too obscure, particularly when thickened with rum or ganja.

At the end of three days I handed them over to my man in Montego Bay. He unravelled them and took them straight off to the Prime Minister's office. The poor sap. He thought the tapes were conclusive proof that the well-connected man in Kingston was up to no good. 'Look Mr Prime Minister,' he said triumphantly. 'This man has to go. If you do fire him I'll take on the job myself.' And he sits back and waits to be patted on the back and promoted. Some hope!

Before you could say 'dope', he was shown the door and I had been given three days to quit the island. I suppose I had become a victim of rum, sun and too much polo. I hadn't noticed the inordinate number of wealthy fat cats with no visible means of support. And I should have never meddled in the politics of Jamaica. It was a daft thing to do. The final irony was that I was already booked on a flight on 28 December and the person who'd made the booking was Pat Seaga. Pat ran a travel agency in Montego Bay. She was also the Prime Minister's sister and I played badminton with her once a week. The terms of my expulsion order were that I had to be out on 23 December, just two days before Christmas.

Christmas isn't just Christmas in the Miller household. It's my wife's birthday too. And this would have been my first Christmas with my new family. 'Aw c'm on guys, give us a break.' But no, there was nothing doing. They wanted me off the island before Christmas. At the time I was really pissed off. It looked as if fate had expelled me from paradise, and I'd never be allowed back. However, I went back in for the Christmas holidays of 1987 and I had no hassle. That may have been incompetence, or it may have been good manners or forgiveness. I'm not inquiring too closely.

Jamaica would have been a good place to spend the second half of my life which, in my early forties, has, I admit, just begun. I've enjoyed the first half and I've had some amazingly good times. Now, maybe, I should settle down. Sarah and I have bought a house in the middle of the English countryside. It's in the heart of Wiltshire. Executive Security is still in operation. The office has moved from Soho to Hammersmith and we still get lots of offers but I've become a little more selective now. However, if I ever got the correct line on Lord Lucan, the temptation to be off would be irresistible . . .

I think of my old school friends, prosperous, dull and slothful in Motherwell and I remember how I always said that would never be the life for me. It wasn't then and it isn't now. There's always going to be another challenge.